YOU'RE ALREADY WORKING

YOU'RE ALREADY WORKING

Here Is Your Creative Practice

Wendy Richmond

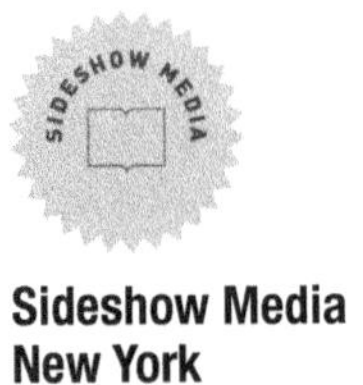

Sideshow Media
New York

ISBN: 978-0-9788143-2-8

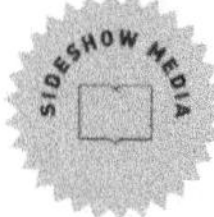

Sideshow Media LLC
www.sideshowbooks.com
Printed and bound in the United States of America

Cover and interior design by Wendy Richmond
Page composition by Corinda Cook

For my brother

CONTENTS

Introduction

1
Place

2
Process

3

Protection

Introduction

One winter, my studio was in a converted barn with thick wooden floors, expansive white walls, and—bolted above a paint-stained sink—an old metal rotary pencil sharpener. I bought a pack of No. 2 pencils at the local dollar store, just so I could use this old relic. One by one, the pencils got stuck, chewed up, and mangled. The first looked like a dog's furry snout, the next like a haystack. They were broken, but beautiful. I taped them to the wall.

Throughout my life, unassuming details like these—a place, an object, a loss—stayed with me, physically or emotionally, inadvertently influencing my creative work. Those ruined pencils alerted me to the power of brokenness. A row of bright yellow taxicabs insisted that I introduce color. A single wave of warm, humid air called my attention to the sense of touch. A teacher's harsh remark forced me to rebuild my trust in my pursuits.

Think back to the early stages of a project of your own. Were there encounters or artifacts that, in retrospect, contributed to the outcome? A child's drawing, a torn glove, a traffic jam, a conversation? Something that anyone else would have discarded or forgotten, but you held onto? Then, finally, its essence found its way into a new painting, a song, a performance, a poem.

You were already working.

My mom often told me that I was lucky because I had an important possession: my work. By that, she did not mean a job or a profession or even a talent. She meant a way of seeing, an intuitive acceptance of what was valid, insistent, and necessary in my art making life. We didn't know what to call it back then, but she was describing my creative practice.

What is a creative practice? It is a foundation of activities and experiences that nurtures an artist's work and solidifies their identity as a creative maker. It has two primary components: One is a commitment to exercises that keep the artist in shape and improve their craft, like attending regular drawing sessions, experimenting with different mediums, or employing new technologies. The other component holds the less acknowledged and often hidden activities, like loitering with intention, sharing grief through physicality, or acknowledging prejudices that obscure history's truths.

As artists, we rely on these components. They are crucial for feeding every stage of our art making. Without them, the finished product could not exist.

You're Already Working relies on personal stories, observations, and research to illuminate the creative practice. Forty-nine chapters, selected from thirteen years of my columns in *Communication Arts* magazine, are organized into four thematic sections, each one offering a different lens through which to understand and expand your creative practice.

1. PLACE examines the role of physical environments in shaping and supporting your art.

2. PROCESS describes how you can engage your senses, trust your intuition, and refine your craft through a balance of structure and spontaneity.

3. PROTECTION is an intimate and vulnerable look at navigating personal and collective uncertainty and loss.

4. PEOPLE explores the connections between artists, their audiences, and other creators across time and disciplines.

My goal is to help you recognize and strengthen your unique creative practice. You will continue to cultivate it and grow it, and you will strive, consciously and unconsciously, to live by it. It is the foundation for making your most meaningful work.

Have courage. Have confidence.

You're already working.

1
PLACE

In every neighborhood where I have lived, there was at least one place that I would visit when I needed to clear out worrisome thoughts. What was it about each site that provided the comfort? What allowed me to leave feeling differently from when I arrived?

Housing the Muse

There are buildings with interior spaces that take my breath away. The Rothko Chapel in Houston, for example, and the Isabella Stewart Gardner Museum in Boston. Also, Frank Lloyd Wright's Fallingwater in southwest Pennsylvania. In each of these places, I feel inspired. As soon as I walk in, the everyday thoughts I had before crossing the threshold are vaporized, and suddenly my head is open: clean and ready to receive something fresh.

In his book *Why Architecture Matters*, Paul Goldberger writes, "We talk about [architectural] spaces in terms of how they feel. It is a sense of awe and contentment, somehow joined, and you feel as if you have been jolted into a higher level of perception than you normally have."

How does this happen? How does a constructed space cause these emotions? As I reflect on the many different places that elevate me to this "higher level," I realize that each building exemplifies a unique aspect of what it means to be inspired.

When I walk into the New York Public Library, it is almost impossible for me to rush through the entrance hall. Its massive arches and grand staircases demand that I take a moment to stop, breathe, and shed the chaotic frenzy of Forty-Second Street.

I met with David Christie, a specialist in the library's Print

Collection, to talk about the space he worked in. When I told David that I have a visceral response to certain architectural spaces, he explained, "When visiting a museum or, in this case the library, one is going to a place that is set aside for communing with the muses ('museum,' meaning temple of the muses), and one adjusts one's mind to be open to receiving what the muses have wrought."

Carrère and Hastings, the library's architects, created a spatial experience; through its sheer scale, its ornament, its placement far from the street, and the interior feeling of expansiveness and openness, the building is set apart from day-to-day routines. The entrance hall is a massive buffer, its main purpose to prepare you to enter the library itself. It is, as David said, a space devoted to clearing your mind, readying it for what the muses have to offer.

Most people are inspired by nature. I am, too, but I am even more inspired when nature is masterfully framed. As Louis Kahn said, "The sun never knew how great it was until it hit the side of a building."

The Pantheon in Rome is an exquisite example. Goldberger writes about the great circular temple: "You don't want to move. To move is to break the spell. What is supposed to move, you realize, is the light, which comes into the space through the oculus, the round opening at the top of the dome."

During a trip to Rome, I stayed in the Albergo del Senato overlooking the Piazza della Rotonda, and I visited the Pantheon regularly. On my last day, as I was about to check out, I glanced out the window and noticed a passing rain shower. Without a second thought, I ran down the stairs, across the piazza, and into the rotunda, just in time to watch the rain as it came through the oculus and turned into mist before it reached the floor.

When I am inspired, I feel a momentum, an urgency to create. I use everything around me to aid in the process. Like a chef in the middle of creating a new dish, I grab what I need, and I don't stop to clean up along the way.

I took a sculpture class years ago at the Carpenter Center at Harvard University. I loved the course, but I was intimidated by the space: The Carpenter Center is Le Corbusier's only building in the United States. It's hard to be unrestrained with your materials when you are wary of doing damage to a famous place, let alone standing aside so that architecture tourists can shoot pictures.

The studio I had in an old mill building by the Charles River, outside of Boston, was the opposite of precious. Unlike the Corbusier building, there was nothing that could not be hammered into, splattered upon, gouged out, or hung from. Its sixteen-foot-tall ceilings, seven-inch-thick floor, and mammoth wooden pillars all said, "Use me."

Recently, I looked up the etymology of the word "inspire." I found this: "c.1300, immediate influence of God, *inspirare* 'inspire, inflame, blow into,' from 'in' + spirare, 'to breathe.'" Perhaps I should rephrase the first line of this chapter and say instead, "There are buildings with interior spaces that breathe into me."

Places
of
Solace

When my dad started to get sick, I was living part-time in La Jolla. On most of the days I was there, I drove to the Salk Institute. If you are interested in Louis Kahn's architecture, you've seen photographs of this site, most likely taken from the beginning of the long stream that cuts through the middle of its wide-open courtyard and heads straight toward the horizon.

The first day I went, I told the guard at the parking lot that I worked at the Institute, and I showed him my camera. From then on, he just waved me in. But the truth is, I didn't work there, and I hardly ever touched my camera. I had come for solace.

I'm not the praying type. The only time I attend a religious service is out of respect for someone else. But, from time to time, when I am troubled, I do seek out places that make me feel better. In every neighborhood where I have lived, whether for a few months or ten years, there was at least one place that I would visit when I needed to clear out worrisome thoughts. What was it about each site that provided the comfort? What allowed me to leave feeling differently from when I arrived?

Like many people, I'm calmed by being in nature—bare feet in sand, a sun bath in a meadow. But for me, the sensation is deepened when nature is honored by an exquisite frame.

For a period when I first lived in Cambridge, my life revolved around the Massachusetts Institute of Technology (MIT). There were times when school, work, and relationships collided, and I needed to escape it all, even for just a few minutes. The MIT chapel, designed by Eero Saarinen, is at the center of the campus; it's a brick cylinder encircled by ashallow moat. There are no windows, and when you're inside, you don't see the moat itself. But there is glass above it, so when the sunlight hits the water, the reflections glow on the cylinder's interior wall.Sometimes I would go to the chapel and watch the light.

During my visits to the Salk Institute, I must have walked on every inch of the courtyard. I rarely sat still, but if I did, I perched on a stone bench and let my eyes follow the stream's flow. One day, workers were making repairs, and the path was bone dry. The loss of this small movement was palpable.

When I was living in Boston's Back Bay, warm evenings called for a stroll to the Christian Science Plaza, in particular to the 700-foot-long reflecting pool, designed by I.M. Pei & Partners and Araldo Cossutta, Associate Architects. If it had been a tough day, I would go three or four times around the perimeter, growing calmer with each lap. Like my visits to the Salk Institute, part of my solace came from my own movement. But again, it was also the outside movement that would hold my focus and soothe me. If there was no wind, the surface of the shallow pool was smooth. Then a tiny breeze would come along, and the water would become new and change everything.

I discovered the New York Zen Center for Contemplative Care the first week I moved to Brooklyn. The meditation schedule was posted on the door. I was feeling unsettled by my move, and this seemed like a promising outlet. The large, tranquil room where *zazen* was practiced was light enough to find an empty spot to sit, but dark enough so that I could feel invisible. One of the reasons I moved to that neighborhood was its sense of community. But what I needed when I went to the Zen Center was to be ignored.

A friend of mine grew up in Kankakee, Illinois, on the cul-de-sac where Frank Lloyd Wright built two of his first Prairie houses. When my friend had his typical teenage tantrums, he would storm out of his house and power walk to the Wright houses, sit down on the curb across the street, and just stare at them until his temper subsided. He says now that in retrospect, looking at Wright's architecture gave him a sense of balance. But I think there was another aspect. These houses, and the curb on which he sat, were just down the street, always available, never hidden or off-limits. Sometimes a requirement for gaining tranquility is knowing that its source will be there.

In the chapter "Housing the Muse," I described physical spaces that inspire me to be creative, where the everyday thoughts I had before crossing the threshold get vaporized, leaving my brain clean and ready to receive something fresh.

Perhaps places of solace are not so different.

Hide and Reveal

Philip Johnson's Glass House in New Canaan, Connecticut, opened to the public in 2007. The guided tour covers a portion of the forty-seven acres and fourteen structures on the estate, including the Glass House itself. The tour allows small groups and is only available during a few months of the year. When I finally got a reservation, it was on a cool autumn day, and the trees were starting to thin out, exposing more of the landscape.

I had come, like most visitors, to be inside the Glass House. I wanted to experience what I had always heard about: a building where the distinction between interior and exterior disappears; walls do not exist; and you can see everything, inside and outside, all at once.

Instead, from the moment we entered the estate, the guide emphasized Johnson's ever-present concept of "hide and reveal." She pointed out the ways that Johnson designed what he called "events on the landscape," and then quoted from an essay by Dorothy Dunn, the former director of Visitor Experience and Fellowships: "The experience of the Glass House is a sequence of choreographed moments, shaped by design, that engage your senses as you move through and between architecture and the landscape." Johnson referred to the estate as his "fifty-year diary"; everything from the Glass House to the pathways, the sculpture, the pool, the Brick House, the Painting Gallery, the Library/Study—even the pruning of the trees—was considered by Johnson to be part of his "organization of procession."

In the chapter "Housing the Muse," I wrote about the feeling of inspiration that architecture can elicit: how the interior spaces of, for example, grand libraries and museums have been designed to remove us from the day-to-day, clearing the mind so that it is open and receptive, "readying it for what the muses have to offer." On my train ride home from the Glass House tour, I thought about why I felt inspired. Throughout the afternoon, I had been engaged in a sort of active loop, repeatedly clearing my mind and then filling it with what the muse, i.e., Philip Johnson, had to offer. But there was something else: I kept coming back to the notion of "hide and reveal," and I realized that I was moved by mystery.

In their book *Cognition and Environment*, the research psychologists Stephen and Rachel Kaplan described the factors that affect how we feel about landscapes. They wrote about the positive value of mystery: "The more preferred scenes are very likely to give the impression that one could acquire new information if one were to travel deeper into the scene. Mystery involves the inference that one could learn more through locomotion and exploration."

Moving through the Glass House estate, whether I was eagerly walking on the curved path for my first glimpse of the Glass House, or coming upon the shocking-blue swimming pool, I was constantly receiving new information. I had entered a rhythm of anticipation, confident that beyond each hill, or behind each structure, or past each stone wall, there would be yet another "event" in Johnson's procession. Each element plays two roles: hiding and revealing. A hill hides and then reveals the Library/Study, which in turn hides and then reveals the Ghost House, and so on. Inside the Painting Gallery, paintings are mounted on rotating panels, so that you see each one by itself, while knowing that there is another one behind it. In the landscape as well as inside the buildings, it is just as exciting to experience the "hide" as it is to experience the "reveal."

There is a park in the Fort Greene neighborhood of Brooklyn that was designed in 1867 by Frederick Law Olmsted and Calvert Vaux, the architects of New York's Central Park and Prospect Park. The day after my visit to the Glass House, I went to the park, reciting the mantra of "hide and reveal" as I came upon each new vista. I enjoyed the surprise of each "unveiling"—the city's skyline, the staircase to the monument at the top of the hill, an outdoor yoga class. Later, I stopped at the Greenlight Bookstore and found an interview with Robert Twombly, editor of *Frederick Law Olmsted: Essential Texts*. Twombly said, "Olmsted didn't think a park should reveal itself in totality from any given place. He thought the park should unfold itself constantly as you walk through it. So there's always a surprise, there's always something new."

Philip Johnson has stated, "Architecture exists only in time. The beauty consists in how you move into the space." It is no surprise that Johnson called Central Park his favorite work of architecture in New York City.

Every
Library
Is
Your
Library

I love to spend time in libraries, whether I'm at home or traveling. One of my favorites is in northern Maine: a tiny, two-room converted cottage with a quirky collection of books and magazines. Another is the Boston Public Library, whose central branch in Copley Square spans an entire city block.

These libraries look like opposites, but they share the qualities that I look for. They provide an atmosphere that is conducive to reading, thinking, exploring, and daydreaming. They are free and open to members of any community, with educational programs for kids and adults. There's accessible technology in a safe space. The librarians are respectful of odd requests, eager to track down something obscure or out of print.

Delivering all these resources is a tall order, whether a library is big or small. But that's just the tip of the iceberg. Because it is open to all, a library must strive to accommodate everyone, without knowing who or what might come through its doors.

A library can't control the filters that each of us brings—filters of age, gender, race, religion, education, geography, politics, and more. But it must be cognizant of these filters, because the only way we can feel comfortable and accepted is if we are seen as individuals.

The best example I know of a library that embraces this ambition is the Jefferson Market Library (JML), the Greenwich Village branch of the New York Public Library. The building—a High Victorian Gothic gem—was originally a courthouse, completed in 1877. A permanent installation by artist Mark John Smith, titled *The Reading Room* (2017), honors the library's fiftieth anniversary.

During a two-year residency, Smith, commissioned by Branch Manager Frank Collerius, designed and implemented the massive installation that covers the walls of the second-floor reading room: a 360-degree, three-story-high print consisting of archival material from patrons' written correspondence dating back to the library's opening.

Fragments of patrons' handwritten letters and notes—from children's scrawls to grownups' cursive script—were scanned at a resolution of 64,000 DPI, showing vibrant details of smudges and fingerprints. The giant letters run sideways up each wall, above the shelves of books; to read them, you turn your head, the same way you do when you peruse the lined-up spines of books. Smith's design employs the upward movement of the soaring and imposing architecture, but uses the personal words to make the room warm and inviting.

When you see the phrases on the wall, you immediately notice that each begins with "I."

"I had the guts to listen"
"I'm one of the lucky"
"I will not lose another book"
"I see you're holding a lecture on"
"I am out of work and cannot afford to buy"

Smith explained, "As a viewer, in your mind you are the I." In a space that caters to the communal public, the individual is illuminated.

The library's responsibility to the individual was also addressed downstairs in JML's lobby, in a temporary installation by the artist Ann Messner titled *the free library and other histories*. It included a twenty-page tabloid, available free to the public, that cites over one hundred references dating from 1833 through 2017 regarding issues such as censorship, privacy, and segregation. Entries range from acts of Congress to Supreme Court rulings, to resolutions adopted by the American Library Association—all pertaining to the library's role in serving individual citizens, regardless of who they are, what they seek, or where they come from.

One of the entries refers to the main character in James Baldwin's 1953 novel *Go Tell It on the Mountain*. Baldwin describes his character's encounter with the Forty-Second Street branch of the New York Public Library: "... a building filled with books and unimaginably vast, and which he had never yet dared to enter. . . . it must be full of corridors and marble steps, in the maze of which he would be lost and never find the book he wanted. And then everyone, all the white people inside, would know that he was not used to great buildings, or to many books, and they would look at him with pity."

We could stop there, knowing that even though the library had its doors open, ready in its mission to serve anyone, it could not control life's realities. But Baldwin continues, "He would enter on another day, when he had read all the books uptown, an achievement that would, he felt, lend him the poise to enter any building in the world."

Alone in Public

On the B train in New York City one morning, I sat next to a woman who had a huge, droopy leather purse open on her lap. She pushed around its contents and retrieved a tiny tube of beige foundation and patted its liquid under each eye. Then she dug deeper into the bag and pulled out an eyelash curler (a scary thing to use on the subway), followed by mascara, blush, and lipstick. Throughout the entire procedure, she seemed oblivious to everything and everyone in the subway car. Music leaked out of her earbuds, the soundtrack to her separate and solitary world.

Every day, millions of urbanites venture out, each of us occupying a tiny piece of communal space. We are simultaneously inhabiting a *non*-physical space: a private, mental zone that surrounds each of us when we are alone in public. These zones are shaped by us, and by whatever is around us.

At times, we want to retreat from public space, and tone down, if not negate, the city's intrusive behavior of noise and grittiness. So we create a "personal bubble," immersing ourselves in private activities that take us away from our current physical surroundings. We turn our focus inward, entering our own worlds: We text, read, listen to podcasts, play games, solve crossword puzzles.

Sometimes the retreat we seek is not from the city's bad

behavior, but from its relentless vibrancy. When I told a friend that I was working on a project about the personal bubble a look of recognition crossed her face. "Oh yes," she said, "We need personal bubbles to protect ourselves." She did not mean protection from terrorists or muggers, but instead from intensity. She said that when she lived in New York, she would often leave her glasses at home so she could deal with the overload. "There's too much to see, to hear, to feel," she said. "By not wearing my glasses, I blur the city's sharpness."

Yet there are times when it is exactly that sharpness that we relish, and then we create a mental zone of total attentiveness, where every sight and sound is a reward. Instead of retreating, we want to be totally present. Unlike my glasses-less friend, this zone is in sharp focus, where all our senses are on high alert. We don't want to miss anything, and at every moment there is something new that we might miss. After the woman who was applying her makeup got off the subway car, she was replaced by three guys drumming, who in turn made way for a dozen harnessed, hand-holding toddlers.

In his book *In Motion*, Tony Hiss describes an experience he calls "deep travel". Hiss encourages his readers to experience what is innate in each of us: the ability to be (and to *enjoy* being) highly responsive to where we are, whether it is a trip far from home, or a walk in our own neighborhood. "Deep Travel," he writes, "has the feeling of waking up further while already fully awake." It occurs, he continues, because of "the awareness we are training on the world around us. This puts us in the position . . . of expecting to find out still more about the things and people around us. . . . it extends both to objects and subjects we ordinarily find fascinating and to those previously thought dull or trivial."

The personal bubble and deep travel are mental states that we cultivate—consciously and unconsciously—when we spend time alone in the urban landscape. A city is a place of extremes, and all its qualities, good and bad, have a flip side. Because of, and in spite of, what the city offers up, we love it. We just have to be in the right state of mind.

When
in
Rome

When I arrived at the American Academy in Rome, I had a brief attack of studio-envy; the artists' workspaces are expansive, with high ceilings and warm Roman light. But I had deliberately chosen not to have a studio; the purpose of my brief month as a visiting artist was to be out and about in the city, observing Rome's version of the personal bubble—the private space that urban dwellers occupy when they are alone in public.

I set out to find the Roman equivalent of the places where I had experienced the personal bubble in New York. I started with the most mundane: the Metro, Rome's underground subway system. Any station would do; I chose the closest, Piramide, and I got on a train headed towards Rebibbia. Right away, the personal bubble was in full display, and I felt like I was on the subway in New York or, for that matter, any other city whose subway I had ridden. The subway car was filled mostly with people who were alone, immersed in their cell phones, books, and newspapers, or simply staring into space; they were retreating into their private cocoons.

I had my new camera with me, and I was prepared to document the evidence. But each time I tried to shoot, the camera lens became a magnet, pulling the riders' focus to me, and their inward gaze became decidedly outward. Their bubbles were invaded and disrupted. The very experience I was trying to capture was pierced by my action.

My next outing to track the personal bubble was a visit to the recently renovated Vatican Library. I wanted to find the Roman version of my experience in grand libraries of other cities, where I've spent many solitary hours next to fellow readers and writers, all of us immersed in our own individual worlds of thoughts, pictures, and words. Gaining entry to the Vatican Library is not easy; it requires a letter of introduction and a considerable amount of time spent waiting at various points inside Vatican City. But once I was in, I came across the quintessential manifestation of the personal bubble.

It was inside the Manuscript Reading Room, where about forty scholars were packed together at long tables, each studying a huge ancient manuscript that was propped carefully on a wooden stand. I stood in the doorway (I had not gotten permission to enter this room), watching the scholars as they turned the precious pages. It was as though there was a protective zone around each body and its manuscript. Every individual's absorption guaranteed that no one would trespass into the other's mental or physical territory.

Cameras were not allowed, so I tried to absorb the scene as best I could, hoping to record this perfect expression of the personal bubble, if only with my eyes. I was practically scanning each person one by one, until my intrusive behavior was noticed, and I was politely shooed away. Once again, my own presence prevented me from getting the evidence.

I left the library frustrated. How was I going to bring home examples of the personal bubble if my attempts at documentation kept disrupting it?

I decided to take a break from my mission and instead indulge in being a tourist. I was in one of the most treasure-filled cities in the world, and it was time to witness its beauty. And so I went to Rome's churches. In one week, I saw Michelangelo's *Moses* in San Pietro in Vincoli, Caravaggio's *The Calling of Saint Matthew* in San Luigi dei Francesi, Cavallini's 13th-century mosaics in Santa Maria in Trastevere . . . the list goes on. Late one afternoon, after eight hours on my feet and nearly back to the Academy, but too tired to face the final hill, I stopped in at the Church of San Pietro in Montorio to rest. I sat down in a pew, leaned back, and closed my eyes. I fell into a dreamy state, and suddenly became aware that someone was in the pew behind me. I felt the presence move closer, perhaps kneeling. Was she praying? Was she even aware of me? I realized that I was observing a personal bubble that was probably more intense than any I had ever seen, and my eyes were closed.

I went back to the church the next day. I waited until I was the only person there, and then I took out my camera and photographed the two pews, now empty. The photograph I brought back home was not a literal documentation of the personal bubble that I had witnessed. But perhaps it was more accurate to capture the memory. No one was there to intrude.

My Roaming Studio

I'm at Gorilla Coffee working. It's 7:45 a.m. and I'm sipping my half-caf two-percent latte that Kyle started making when he saw me crossing the street. As I write, I also respond to emails, peruse relevant blogs, shoot a video of a truck outside with weird typography, and post it for my students. I tap Shazam to find out what crazy music Kyle has chosen (The Mars Volta: "Drunkship of Lanterns") to wake the place up.

It's a productive morning in my roaming studio.

In 1995, I wrote an essay titled "Digital Napkins." At the time, companies were "downsizing," and designers were freelancing and "telecommuting," buzzwords that were precursors of the mobile way we work now. A phenomenon called cybercafés was popping up: places with couches next to computers. People were working—alone and together—in public spaces. I was excited about the idea of a more mobile and fluid workplace, one that was born out of the intersection of the digital and physical worlds.

Since that time, my workspaces have ranged in size (from a thousand-square-foot barn to a tiny cell phone screen) and location (from San Diego to Rome), and regardless of square footage and place, I have continued to crave and seek out the creative energy that comes from working in public.

In a roaming studio, I am working alone, but I'm not isolated. I'm engulfed in an ocean of communities, always surging and changing. My physical community is made up of fellow café-mates, often sitting for hours, our faces illuminated by our screen portals. My digital community is more staccato, coming and going in texts, emails, and posts. Both of these realms straddle a balance between companionship and anonymity, between being deep in thought and sliding into conversations with others.

I find my roaming studios in different neighborhoods, cities, and countries. The digital online world is the same, but it is affected by the physical world. In Cambridge, I go to a café near MIT. Tables are crowded with technology: There are more laptops and smartphones than there are people. My occasional eavesdropping sends me googling stock prices. When I was in Rome, the digital component shrank to cell phone only (a laptop felt absurd in an Italian café), and I renewed my love of sketching on paper.

In Brooklyn, my roaming studio depends on the time of day, the weather, or my mood. In the afternoon, I like to go to BRIC, a center for community arts and media. BRIC's building houses two theater spaces, classrooms, a public access TV center, and a three-thousand-square-foot gallery. All of its spaces are wired, with the intention of broadcasting events to Brooklyn households, and beyond.

At the heart of BRIC is a café whose seating spills out to a bleacher-like expanse of wide steps with orange and gray pillows. Stenciled across the steps, in huge letters, is the word STOOP. I sit on the stoop with my laptop, phone, and cappuccino, alternating between working, watching the action, and engaging in conversations. Like the many stoops in the neighborhood, this is where new acquaintances are easily made, a more organic form of networking than social media. BRIC's architects and activities planners understand that its digital and physical communities are not separate and celebrates that in a shared public space.

Of course, the atmosphere of a café is unpredictable, and at any moment an annoying cell phone conversation or a screaming baby can destroy your train of thought. But commotion also offers serendipity and inspiration. Often, it's the constantly evolving partnership of the digital and the physical that provides the fodder for creative work. And sharing peeks into one another's real-time place and process can engender a sense of closeness and collaboration.

After I shot the video of that truck driving by Gorilla's window, I saw a post by one of my students in my video class. I "liked" her video and commented on it with a suggestion about lighting. A minute later, I saw her new post: a short clip using shadows. Another student recorded his own surroundings, playing off the shapes of the previous one, and that got a visual repartee going. It felt like a cross between a classroom critique and an online exquisite corpse. There I was in my roaming studio, and my students were roaming in it.

In his book *A Moveable Feast*, Ernest Hemingway describes the way he works on a story. Often, he's alone in a café, and a conversation or detail of someone's face finds its way into his notebook. I like to think of my roaming studio—public and private, digital and physical—as a 21st-century moveable feast.

My
Studio
Wall

Within the first few days of my residency at MacDowell, I learned that it was perfectly okay to draw and write and nail things on the vast white walls of my studio. With this simple permission, plus a ladder, hammer, Magic Markers, and pushpins, every idea I had went onto the wall without judgment or hesitation. As its space filled, the wall became not only a physical artwork itself, but also a metaphor for my creative process: All ideas are worthy of being made visible.

I had come to MacDowell to begin a new body of visual work. I was replacing my dense, urban, technology-laden Brooklyn environment with a spacious, solitary, internet-free studio in the middle of 450 acres of snowy New Hampshire woods. Now I faced, literally, a huge blank canvas.

My first day with the wall began timidly: In pencil, tiny and at eye level, I wrote, "Starting here." Then I told myself it was just a wall, and my goal was simply to fill it. I climbed to the top of the ladder and wrote out every word of my most recent essay, "What Do You Do with Beauty?" I climbed back down and felt the satisfaction of having physically filled a chunk of wall. As I reread the words, I remembered a discussion with friends about how we all interpret beauty differently, and under the essay, I scrawled, "Odd Beauty: Think about it."

Next, I moved to the middle of the wall, where I made a list of themes that I wanted to explore: new technology/old technology; urban/rural; frozen/melted; pristine/spoiled; frustration/success.

I sat down and noticed the pencil I had first used. I had sharpened it, along with six others, with the old-school metal rotary pencil sharpener that was mounted above the sink, and I'd mangled them badly: Some were cracked and split; others were shredded and looked furry, like a dog with a lead snout. I taped the pencils to the wall and drew an arrow to the words "Odd Beauty". Then I shot a close-up of the broken wood and enlarged it tenfold. That, too, went on the wall. Later in the day, I went for a walk and found frozen puddles, which I videotaped as I crunched them with my boots. I printed pictures of single video frames of beautiful cracked ice patterns and tacked them on the wall near the list of themes. I drew more arrows. I was off and running.

By the second week, the wall was populated with notes, sketches, photographs, and objects, all having conversations and making connections. This spurred more observations, which led to more video recording, more picture taking, more writing. The volume of stuff, and its visual exuberance, inspired me. Because of the growing abundance, no single item had too much pressure; it was like a community of individuals there to support one another.

I was feeling more playful than I had in years. Joy, humor, and physicality took full command of my work. I started a new list, titled: "What can I do in this studio that I can't do anywhere else?" (Item #5: "Dance, big and loud, before dawn.") The list grew, encouraging and challenging me to see everything in my surroundings as creative fodder. (Item #7: "Draw a target and practice throwing snowballs.")

During my third week, the visual artists decided to have an open studio walk to see each other's studios. I was anxious; I would be exposing this wall that had been for my eyes only. But all fears evaporated when I saw the glee of my colleagues (including writers, filmmakers, and composers), and heard them say, "Wow! I want to do this on my wall!" Yes, they were looking at what I had created, but what they were really seeing was the concept and practice of making all ideas visible. Then they looked at my target. We ran outside and collected snow, and one by one, a dozen of us threw snowballs in my studio. The wall soaked up the laughter, and it stayed with me.

Taken separately, each of my wall activities might seem like a crazy, silly diversion having nothing to do with "real work." But every day, as I sat with a cup of coffee and let my eyes scan the wall, I learned more about my art making. Not only was I seeing connections, I was also allowing spontaneity and freedom to guide the work. By making all ideas visible, I was letting them lead the way.

Discovering Your Workspace Mojo

I have a collection of smooth black stones on the windowsill in my studio. When I'm in the middle of a project, I spend time at the window, absentmindedly pushing the stones around. I hadn't thought about the shapes I was making until one day, after snapping a picture of a spectacular sunset, I noticed that the stones were in a series of neat lines and spirals. Seeing a photograph of this unconscious, yet deliberate, arrangement made me realize that I perform a ritual—a tactile meditation—as part of my creative process.

The physical contents of our workspaces, and the ways we arrange and interact with them, can have a powerful and often overlooked effect. After my newly discovered relationship with my stones, I wanted to pursue this question: Are we aware of the ways that our workspaces—and all the stuff that lives within them—nourish our creative mojo?

Photography is a well-known method for seeing what we tend to overlook, so I asked friends to send me pictures of their workspaces. I was seeking physical evidence of the elements and rituals that support a balance of productivity and inspiration.

The first photos I received were from a writer, showing the expected fundamentals: desk, chair, computer, phone, printer, books, and a cup full of pens and pencils. But then I noticed, next to the desk, a rumpled bed with two big pillows. I figured it was for napping, but when I asked my friend, she responded, "I hadn't thought about this before, but I have a specific body position for each stage of my writing. I lie on the bed to read catalogs and books for my research. My actual writing takes place at my desk, and when I reach the later stages, I read my final drafts on the bed, but this time with my head at the opposite end."

A programmer/designer friend works in his Manhattan high-rise apartment; he chose the place for its floor-to-ceiling windows, each one filled with Midtown's density. He, too, has the requisite computer (or two or three), phone, printer, a jar of pens, and so on. But his primary desk is a large table where he spreads out a precise grid of index cards covered with intricate, color-coded notations. I was already familiar with his process, but when I looked at the photographs he sent me, each one carefully composed to show both his table and the view from his windows, I was struck by the similarity of his grid of index cards to the grid of the city's buildings. I may be reading too much into this, but it was impossible to ignore the way he infused his workspace with his particular kind of visual thinking.

A multimedia designer sent me pictures of her boyfriend's studio. He is an artist who creates meticulous, detailed illustrations. His space is a giant Joseph Cornell box: Each surface holds an installation. Hundreds of objects are organized with careful attention to texture, shape, color, and size: a white lace tablecloth under a dark watercolor of two skulls; hunting knives beside an antique globe; driftwood next to a toy model of a Lamborghini; a ram's horns on a rickety bookshelf. My friend had been admonishing her boyfriend to work more, to be "more productive." But after taking the photographs, she realized that his workspace is teeming with productivity: ongoing activities that are elaborate works in progress, all integral to the development and meaning of his paintings.

I love receiving these photographs; they show the similarities as well as the uniqueness of people's items and habits. An architect's studio includes a wall unit filled with skeins of knitting yarn and a sweater in progress on an Eames chair. An animator's workstation is tucked into the corner of a tiny bedroom; her dog sprawls by the desk, and her two cats are curled up on an overstuffed armchair.

One friend, an artist whose work is abrasive and political, sent a photo that showed his studio's marked absence of artifacts. There is a computer on a slab of wood, balanced on Home-Depot-style sawhorses, plain walls, no windows. There is nothing personal other than a half-full plastic container of trail mix. Though he has occupied the studio for years, the space conveys the feeling that some anonymous entity has flown in and might leave at any moment.

All these photographs have shown me each individual's inclination to shape, quite literally, their creative practice, whether it's collecting artifacts, performing rituals, or removing all extraneous matter. What would a photograph of your workspace reveal?

A Studio at Home?

So far in this century, I've had eight studios. I have loved each one, but circumstances always cut the affair short: a cross-country move, a landlord who wanted the space for himself, a takeover by CubeSmart, and, finally, COVID-19.

My last studio was large, bright, and convenient—just one stop away from home on the express train. But when the pandemic hit, and then worsened, I couldn't get there safely. By the summer, after metaphorically shoveling rent money into a garbage can, I decided to forfeit my security deposit and cancel my lease.

During COVID-19, I hibernated in three different cities and towns, downsizing my studio practice to an iPad. When COVID-19 finally receded and I was fully vaccinated, it was time to venture out and look for a studio. But faced with the all-too-familiar prospect of an exhausting search, an exorbitant rent, and an unpredictable commute, I'm considering something new: Could I have a studio at home?

Obviously, it would be great to be free from the headaches of renting a studio. But I don't want to move forward by avoiding negatives. I want to *want* a different space. How can I make a home studio as good as, if not better than, my former studios?

First, I need to honor my studio practice as an essential activity in my home. If you browse online for "art studios at home," it's mostly about the poor cousin: the basement, the attic, a corner of the kitchen. What if, instead of the worst space, I pick the best? In my apartment, that's the primary bedroom, so that will be the studio. (Fortunately, I live alone, so there's no conflict.)

My first studio was a coming of age: I was giving myself permission to live the life I desired. I signed a lease, I paid rent, I took two buses to get there. Since then, I've adhered to the belief that I needed to "go somewhere else" to make my art.

Could the opposite be true? Instead of separating work and home, could I integrate them? One of my favorite displays at the Metropolitan Museum of Art is the Studiolo from the Ducal Palace in Gubbio, Italy. A Renaissance studiolo reflected its owner's ideals, and was a place for contemplation, reading, and lively discussions with visitors. In my apartment, I want to reimagine the living room as a studiolo. It will hold all my books, and its walls will be a changing display of art and artifacts—mine, friends', and other works I've collected. The objective is to bring my practice—its process and inspirations—into every room.

I've always felt that a studio should be raw and ready to accept hammering, gouging, and splattering. Yes, I can design my home studio to be nonprecious, with a floor that permits spilling and walls that invite tacking up. But it won't be the same kind of freedom I had in my industrial spaces. How do I ensure that I won't be curtailed? Ironically, during the last two decades, some of my messiest work was made outside of my studio. For an etching project, I joined Robert Blackburn Printmaking Workshop, where I used a platemaker and an etching press. I started a letterpress and photo series at a month-long residency at Women's Studio Workshop and then worked with a letterpress printer to complete the portfolio. I'm confident that exploring resources outside of the studio will expand rather than shrink my work.

Each of my studios has been a sanctuary, a place of solitude. But as we learned during the pandemic, what starts as solitude can turn into isolation. I will miss the beehive of a bustling artists' building and the spontaneity of meeting my neighbors in the hallway. Finding and maintaining a community will require attention. In the past, workshops, residencies, and drawing groups have provided camaraderie; many led to collaborations. These activities have always been part of my practice, and hopefully, that won't change.

When I discuss my potential plan with friends, they describe their own studios. The range is extreme, but the common denominator is having a space that supports total immersion in their creative process. My goal is the same.

Habits of Home

My eyes tend to get dry, so my ophthalmologist recommended a twice-daily regimen that includes wearing a warm compress over both eyes for eight minutes. Fine, but what should I do for those sightless eight minutes, twice a day? I was in the planning stage of renovating my apartment, so I decided to try an experiment: I would use my sense of touch to get a new perspective on the way I inhabit my living space.

After fastening the compress to my head, I start my expedition. I run my hand along the table and find a tangle of power cords. I grasp the handle of a closet door, and I'm pleased by its smooth shape. I feel the wooden school desk that I've cherished for years and a poorly placed cabinet that threatens to hit me in the face.

When I take off the compress, I look around with fresh (and less dry) eyes, and I see, with new awareness, other examples of my attentiveness and negligence, my delights and letdowns.

I invite you to join me in thinking about how we design—consciously and unconsciously—our domestic spaces. Have you made small adjustments, like replacing a showerhead? Or big changes, like moving from a one-bedroom apartment in the city to a cottage in the country? And conversely, what desires did you not act upon because you did not have (a) the wherewithal; (b) the energy; or (c) the courage? Like my touch-only encounters around my home, we begin with literal surfaces, but when we dig deeper, we reveal more.

For the first four months of the pandemic, I lived at my best friend's house. I love being there: It is a visual feast, filled with art and artifacts collected from family members, trips, garage sales, and hobbies. I've often thought I wanted my own home to be more like that. But when I returned to my apartment, I felt good within its comparative emptiness. White space is my preference and always has been. One of my favorite books is *Josef + Anni Albers: Designs for Living*. In it, there's a letter that Josef Albers wrote in 1928 to his friends who were moving. "Now take care and make sure your apartment is clean, light and empty," he advised. On a separate post-card, he exclaimed, "The empty room is the best!!!!!!!!!!!" (I counted the exclamation points; there are eleven!)

During one of my eight-minute room-touching exercises, I opened a drawer full of travel-size bottles and another with toiletry bags. I travel often—sometimes for a couple of days, sometimes for much longer—and I accumulate these to use for my trips. At first, they seem to have nothing to do with my choices regarding domestic space. But looking again, I see that they embody one of the primary reasons I live in a condominium: I can pick up and go without worrying about the upkeep that a house typically demands.

When I seek advice from savvy home renovators, they say I should plan as though I will live in my renovated home for at least twenty-five years years. This makes me consider the impending dwindling of my abilities—in other words, aging. My mom lived to the age of ninety-six, and I had a lot of experience in witnessing, helping with, and learning about the aging process. As she became older and less capable, focused on eliminating potential hazards and difficulties she might encounter. I removed rugs in the hallways, added grab bars in the bathroom, and so on. This was all good, but looking back, I see that her desires were not for safety; instead, they were for many of the same passions that I have—in particular, beautiful design. For example, in another of my walks around my apartment without sight, I came upon a lamp that had belonged to my mom. I had forgotten about its skinny on-off knob. When we saw it in the store, I had worried that it would be challenging for her arthritis, but she wanted it. After it was delivered, she twisted a few rubber bands around the knob and voilà, no problem.

My mom's desires and modifications are lessons for me now: If we focus on hazard-avoiding safeguards for "old age," we may forget to supply ourselves with the very things we have always loved.

Your surroundings might seem like they coalesced by chance, but choices were made, which in turn affected more choices. What do your decisions about your home reveal about how you live now, and what do they suggest for the future?

Where Does Your Work Want to Live?

In 2007, I finalized a series of tiny cell phone videos—hundreds of low-resolution, fifteen-second, surreptitious snippets of urban life. The format consisted of grids of videos looping continuously on small digital monitors. When the series was shown on the spacious walls of a museum, I was thrilled. The silent, dark rooms displayed the work with maximum clarity and minimal distraction.

Fast-forward a few years: I'm in a taxi, stuck in traffic, with no air conditioning, windows open, honking horns, and food truck smells. I watch scenes that are near replicas of my videos: a man running down the stairs to the subway, a woman being pulled by her miniature poodle. Then I notice the taxi's little back seat TV monitor—the same size as the monitors in my exhibition—and it hits me: This is where my videos want to live!

Yes, I want my work to be seen in pristine, controlled settings. But when I imagined the videos looping on the monitor in the taxi, they took on another, parallel life. There, the viewer could simultaneously be a witness and a participant in the frustration and gusto of everyday city life. What better home for my urban choreographies than the back of a taxicab, riding alongside their real-life counterparts?

Since that cab ride, I've asked colleagues and students this question: Where does your artwork want to live? They usually assume that I'm asking which galleries, museums, or publications they want to be shown in. Then I repeat the question and add clarification: I'm not talking about where you want your work to live—I'm asking where *your work* wants to live. Where will it have the most impact? Are there surroundings that will convey its meaning more clearly? Does it want interaction with its viewers? Does it seek an audience outside of the art world?

My sculpture series *Like the Back of My Hand* was four years in the making. In addition to the final sculptures, there were hundreds of broken fragments from the casts of my hands, each one unique and evocative. I like to talk to my work, so I asked these pieces where they wanted to live, and what I "heard" was: "We want to go home with people." The result was an installation at the New York Public Library titled *Check Out This Sculpture*, in which patrons were invited to select, borrow, and return a piece of sculpture, just as they would a library book. By the close of the installation, more than one hundred pieces had lived in people's homes, returning with new stories to tell.

I'm not suggesting that you should pass up a gallery or any other conventional venue. But your artwork's life is long, and an exhibition at a particular location is brief. Over time, your work can live in multiple dwellings. You can honor your art by thinking outside the (white cube) box.

I usually see the work of artists I admire in museums and galleries. But I've also found their art in different, unusual locations, and these experiences have deepened or altered my connection with their work. A new setting could sharpen your awareness of, say, a diverse population, as in Vik Muniz's *Perfect Strangers* series at the Seventy-Second Street subway station in Manhattan. Or it might induce levity—quite literally—as William Wegman's video *Up Down Up* does in the elevator in Denver's the ART, a hotel. A roadside billboard displaying an image by Felix Gonzalez-Torres of an empty, unmade bed with two pillows will stop you in your tracks.

For me, Anthony McCall is a good example of an artist whose work has different effects depending on the environment. My first encounter with his 3-D light sculptures was during a visit to Governors Island in New York. *Between You and I* was part of an exhibition of public artworks presented by the nonprofit arts organization Creative Time. McCall's installation was in the St. Cornelius Chapel, a soaring space designed by Charles C. Haight. The chapel's windows were covered, so the interior was pitch-black—except for two cones of intense light shining down from the high ceiling. Nothing else was visible until a fellow viewer (worshipper?) glided into a cone.

I've seen versions of McCall's work in two other locations: Fundació Gaspar, in Barcelona, and Pioneer Works, in Brooklyn. The Barcelona show, *Solid Light, Performance and Public Works*, was a survey of the artist's work—McCall began his series of solid light works in 1973. I was immersed in the art, but unlike my almost spiritual experience in the chapel, this visit was cerebral. Because of the curator's detailed presentation of McCall's trajectory, I was more inclined to think than to feel.

Pioneer Works is a cultural center whose huge brick building houses residencies, exhibitions, performances, and workshops. Like the St. Cornelius Chapel, the space was completely dark except for the light works. But here, it was crowded with families, couples, and individuals, all noisily interacting with the works, interrupting the hazy light with their hands, bodies, and, of course, smartphones. The high-energy atmosphere was the opposite of the chapel: It was about community, not solitude.

One venue was not "better" than the other; instead, each provided a unique experience that expanded my relationship with McCall's art.

As artists, we're grateful for the opportunity to exhibit in a gallery or museum. But your art—which receives such a huge dose of your creative effort—deserves one more leap of the imagination. So consider finding other homes for it. You may be surprised when your work ventures out of the neighborhood.

Which reminds me of that TV in the taxi. . .

2
PROCESS

First, I immersed myself in a goal-free activity, then I used the discipline of note-taking to investigate it. What did I learn? How did it inform my work?

What Do You Do with Beauty?

There is a mile-long stretch of the Maine coastline that I have come to love; I especially look forward to seeing its splendor change with every season. Last summer, on an early-morning walk, a rainbow appeared. It was all white! I witnessed this exquisite phenomenon with dueling feelings of awe and agitation. Yes, I wanted to simply look at the rainbow, but its beauty also made me want to *do* something with it.

As humans, we have the good fortune to know and appreciate beauty. And alongside that appreciation comes other human traits, such as the need to own, share, protect, and/or create with it. Does that need (and its subsequent action) deepen our connection with beauty, or take away from it? The more I ponder this conflict, the more curious I am about its complexity.

When I saw the white rainbow, my instinct was to pull out my cell phone and take a picture. At first, I felt annoyed at my phone for inserting itself between me and nature. But then I realized that the impulse came from a desire to hold onto and expand my connection, and in this regard, the cell phone was both a culprit and an ally.

In 1998, I wrote a column titled "Visual Episodes," and referred to Susan Sontag's classic book *On Photography.* Sontag describes photographing as a means of attaining ownership: "To collect photographs is to collect the world." She writes, "Photographs really are experience captured, and the camera is the ideal arm of consciousness in its acquisitive mood."

Around the time I wrote my column, I was traveling in Italy, using a point-and-shoot camera to "collect" abstract forms that I found to be uniquely stunning. Not only did I want to have and keep those beautiful forms, I also felt that by making them mine, I developed a heightened awareness of my aesthetic vision. But now, many years later, I wonder: Are my photographs just souvenirs that I acquired during my journey, not unlike the leather gloves and silk scarf I bought while I was there? Did I miss out on truly absorbing beauty because I was determined to take it with me, as opposed to concentrating on the real-time experience?

Ownership (which can be broadly defined) is one way of connecting with beauty. Whether it adds to or subtracts from one's bond is an open question.

In her popular book *Alone Together: Why We Expect More from Technology and Less from Each Other*, Sherry Turkle writes, "Technology makes it easy to express emotions while they are being formed. It supports an emotional style in which feelings are not fully experienced until they are communicated."

On one hand, I see how technology lessens our connection with beauty. Turkle suggests that we need to communicate in order to know what we feel. And so, before we even give ourselves a chance to hold and comprehend beauty, we send it away: We export and expunge it, via text, post, or Instagram. On the other hand, the act of simultaneously seeing and sharing can enrich our appreciation of beauty. When I looked at the rainbow, I knew what I felt: joy! And I wanted to express that to people I care for. I wanted them to have some part of it, and why not right away? So, again, an external tool was poised to be both my aid and my distraction.

Some of our most profound interactions with natural beauty are experienced through works of art. One of my favorite places to see collaborations between artists and the landscape is Storm King Art Center in New Windsor, New York. Sculptures there have been created using natural materials like the native grasses in Maya Lin's *Storm King Wavefield* and the stones in Andy Goldsworthy's *Wall That Went for a Walk*, as well as contrasting materials, like the steel plates of Richard Serra's *Schunnemunk Fork*. We understand beauty through *their* efforts to understand it. As Goldsworthy says, "I'm trying to get beneath the surface appearance of things. Working the surface of a stone is an attempt to understand the internal energy of the stone."

For those of us with art making in our DNA, this collaboration includes the compulsion to make our mark, convey a stance, or perhaps encourage an audience to see something more. However—and here I am speaking for myself—this urge is also presumptuous, an act of hubris. What mark could I make that would not detract from what is perfect, let alone add to it? In this conflict, I always hope that the urgency to connect with beauty is stronger than the fear of thwarting it.

The
Interview
Tool

I was in the local café, my favorite place to write. But the task at hand—constructing a cohesive presentation about my current artwork—was getting nowhere. I had all the visuals, but my attempts to compose the words to accompany them were failing. I suffer from the same problem that many of my fellow visual artists have: Describing my artwork is an agonizing challenge.

So I emailed my friend Susan Hodara, a journalist who has interviewed countless artists for the hundreds of articles she has written about the arts. I asked her for help, and we made a date.

Susan arrived at my studio armed with an audio recorder, a notebook, a list of questions, and her laptop: everything she needed for conducting our interview. We worked the entire afternoon, and by the time Susan left, we had developed language that clearly articulated the concepts for my presentation. By using her well-honed process, Susan was able to extract what I had not been able to verbalize myself.

As an artist, your primary language is a visual one. But there are many times when you need words to support your work—whether for an exhibition catalog, a lecture, a grant proposal, or an artist statement. You've probably found all sorts of how-to guides, but in my experience, these do-it-yourself approaches are not careful investigations. They may provide the aid of a standard blueprint, but they cannot unearth a truly insightful result.

As I think back to my interview with Susan, I see that the steps she used were vital for achieving clear and honest language about my art.

1. Record

Susan turned on her recorder and began asking me questions about my intentions, my inspirations, and the evolution of this particular body of work. As I responded, she pushed me further: "What do you mean?" "Tell me more." "Why?" I had to think hard; I found myself rephrasing my descriptions, adding details I'd overlooked or taking back platitudes I had flippantly spewed. The more we talked, the more excited I became, seeing my work in ways I hadn't before. Susan knew from experience that her questions would help me to illuminate the heart of my work.

2. Transcribe and distill

We completed the interview after an hour or so, and I went for a long walk while Susan transcribed our conversation on her computer. This was no mundane activity; it was her practiced method of absorbing the information I'd shared. "Listening to the interview and typing the words is when I really hear what was being said," she told me. "As I listen, I distill. I notice repeated subjects and key words, and I start to recognize the essence of what's being communicated. I hear statements that are vague or not fully thought through, and statements that feel true and significant. It's not possible to grasp this material during the interview stage. It's only while transcribing that these important aspects arise."

3. Organize

The resulting document was more than a written record. Yes, these were my words, but Susan had organized them into a unified structure. The sentences were cohesive, free of my occasional meandering. There were subheads identifying themes and content: from "Seeds and Sticky Fingers" to "Armor and Drawing" to "Materials and Research." There was a clarity that I had been unable to uncover myself; the pages made my thoughts seem orderly, less daunting than when they'd been spinning around in my brain. I was confident that this would provide a substantial framework for the writing I needed to prepare. Susan emailed me the document and went home.

There were two more steps, and they came from me. The first happened before we actually started: I acknowledged that I needed the skills of a professional and made the request. Susan and I agreed upon specific compensation (happily, a barter) and a dedicated, distraction-free period of time, which helped me to commit to the process.

The other step took place after she left. I reviewed her transcript and pulled out the pieces that I felt would best serve the visuals for my presentation. I had to make changes and clarifications, but instead of being annoyed, I was delighted that I knew what I wanted to modify. Since then, I've mined the transcript repeatedly, for proposals, press releases, and the many occasions when I've had to describe my work.

The "Interview Tool" is not a conversation with a book club buddy or studio-mate or life partner; you need to work with someone who is trained and can use specific expertise. Nor is it about hiring someone to deliver a polished, finished document. Instead, it is an opportunity to engage in a thoughtful, instructive process that will serve you far beyond an immediate task.

Blogging with a Different Perspective

Blog blog blog. Every time I thought about starting a blog, I felt annoyed and guilty. Each new blog I came across increased the pressure to have one of my own. But the task just kept going to the bottom of the to-do list.

At the time, I was working on a multimedia collaboration. My colleagues and I were in the exploratory stage of creating an interactive exhibit, and we each documented our thoughts and research in varied ways: shooting stills and video, recording sound, sketching, scanning, coding, downloading, and writing. After several meetings, as we tried to corral a bunch of random, fast-moving concepts, I surprised myself by saying, "What if we had a blog?"

I began to see a different perspective: Blogging in the original sense ("blog" is a contraction of "web log") could be a tool to foster and reflect upon the development of our work.

Keeping undeveloped ideas from public view is appropriate for traditional forms of publishing and presentation, like a magazine and a gallery. But a blog, because of its nature, gives permission—even encouragement—to share work in progress. One of the toughest battles in the creative process is maintaining a balance between keeping ideas open and making conclusive decisions. I often encourage students, and myself, to hold that balance by showing rough iterations to a circle of trusted colleagues. (If you choose, you can control the reach of your blog's circle.)

The late Agnes Martin said: "The bad paintings have to be painted, and to the artists are more valuable than those paintings later brought before the public." Keeping a log of the so-called bad ideas is a great way to see the evolution of your work. Often, when you look back, you see discarded elements that may now have value. As an educator, I know that the "bad paintings" are important to other people as well. When I go to an exhibit, I always wonder: What was attempted along the way? The rejected work can be illuminating not only for the artist, but also for the audience.

Like most artists, I need to have deadlines and destinations for my work. But even with those two taskmasters, day-to-day progress can be difficult. A blog is a sort of personal trainer. And as I think again about that nagging requirement of having something new for each entry, I remember one of my own basic rules: By seeing what repeats, you discover what has lasting value. A blog lets you fast-rewind and fast-forward—an easy way to see what patterns are emerging in your work.

One of the greatest joys of being involved in an exciting project is that everything seems relevant. Doing the work—whether it is an exhibit, a play, or a book—includes permission to spend time exploring the world around me. But this abundance of input can be overwhelming. How do I keep it all present, let alone organized and accessible?

In her book *The Creative Habit*, choreographer Twyla Tharp describes beginning each new project with a big cardboard box. Everything of any interest—notebooks, news clippings, CDs, pieces of art—goes into the box. Our blog was a receptacle, a multimedia version of Twyla's boxes. It provided a window to many dimensions, because it allowed viewing, listening to, categorizing, sharing, and commenting on the pieces that each of us was creating and collecting.

When we finally installed the exhibit and produced the accompanying catalog, our blogging ended. We no longer needed it. It had served its crucial purpose: providing a powerful support for developing and completing a collaborative multimedia body of work.

Becoming Fluent

I drew often during high school and college, and I've continued sporadically throughout my life. At one point, I decided to be more rigorous with my drawing practice and enrolled in a drawing class. My technique was okay, but I was not proficient. I wanted to improve my rendering skills so that I could whip out fluid, accurate sketches of objects and physical spaces for my videos and installations. I had no intention of exhibiting my drawings; they were intended to support my "real" work.

During that time, I read an article by the novelist Jhumpa Lahiri in *The New Yorker* magazine titled "Teach Yourself Italian." In her piece, Lahiri describes her desire to find another direction for her writing, a new approach. Her long journey of learning Italian was at first intermittent, then grew in intensity, to the point where she wrote a book in her new language. (She has, since then, written and translated numerous articles, books, and essays in Italian.)

Though my immersion into drawing was very different from Lahiri's in scope, intention, and dedication (she moved her family to Rome!), I realized that, like her, I wanted to broaden my approach to my art making. I wanted to become fluent in another language. For me, that language was drawing.

As I read the stages of her quest, I began to see parallels. Lahiri wrote about her early phases of learning: "I'm bound to fail when I write in Italian, but, unlike my sense of failure in the past, this doesn't torment or grieve me."

Each week, I saw my slow but steady improvement. I liked entering a different language, where my only judgment was of my progress. I forgave mistakes easily. Normally, I'm prone to questioning myself—my purpose, my worthiness—as an artist. In the drawing class, I was free from those plaguing thoughts. Instead, my questions were simple: Are the room's angles correct? Am I capturing the model's gestures? Is my pencil sharp enough?

Soon after arriving in Rome, Lahiri begins to write in her diary in Italian. She describes the challenge as groping her way "like a child, like a semiliterate," and then writes, "I don't recognize the person who is writing this diary in this new, approximate language. But I know that it's the most genuine, most vulnerable part of me."

Here I paused. Reading that paragraph, I again had a feeling of recognition, but this time it was not a good one. Like Lahiri, I didn't recognize myself when I was drawing, but it was not because I was finding my vulnerability or genuineness. On the contrary: I seemed to be losing both. As I gained proficiency, I was forfeiting expression.

I decided to look back at drawings I had done years ago, in the late 1990s. They lacked accuracy, but they were more compelling. Each one captured a mood and circumstance—a carefree summer of swimming and sailing, a horrific winter of upheaval. More importantly, they were clearly mine. The drawings I was doing in class were more skilled, but they could be anyone's.

In proclaiming that drawing was not my real work—"I'm just using my sketches for support, I'm just improving my technique"—was I letting myself off the hook? While I rejoiced in my ego-less state, was I using it as an excuse? Yes, I wanted to be free of self-judgment, but not because I had limited my expectations. I removed a burden, but I'm afraid I've also closed a door.

So now I am at a turning point. As I become more fluent, I see the possibility of using drawing as another "language" of visual expression, alongside my other public work of video, photography, and installation. I want to use my new and improved skills and also recover the expressiveness of my old drawings.

At the end of her article, Lahiri writes, "I am, in Italian, a tougher, freer writer, who, taking root again, grows in a different way."

Will I sustain my drawing practice to the point of real fluency? And if I do, will I be able to retain expression and freedom? By allowing my drawings to share the title of real work, I hope they will help me to grow as an artist—maybe even a tougher one.

How Do You Trust Your Intuition?

In the book *Between Artists: Twelve Contemporary American Artists Interview Twelve Contemporary American Artists*, the late Sarah Charlesworth said to fellow photographer Laurie Simmons, "You have a way of working that you call intuitive, and you trust yourself, which is a big thing. . . . That, to me, is very scary—when you decide to trust something working without being able to give an explanation."

I always assumed that Charlesworth, who was an influential and prolific conceptual artist, had no problem relying on her instincts, so I was surprised when she expressed what I have often questioned: What's behind my intuition? I wasn't born with it. I didn't wake up one morning and say, "I know exactly where my work is headed." If I want to make progress, I need to understand the reasons that allow me to trust myself when I say, "It works."

Let's say you're creating a new body of work. The exploration is perhaps more personal (and uncomfortable) than you're accustomed to. In order to move forward and trust your instincts, you first need to illuminate the foundation that supports them.

Your intuition is more developed than you may realize. It has become second nature: You have a built-in vocabulary, a repertoire, a unique voice, a way of communicating. This comes from your technical training and your accumulation of experience and expertise. Even when you take a snapshot, you are unconsciously choosing the lighting, composition, framing; you even consider—again unconsciously—how you will modify it in Photoshop.

In a studio art class years ago, I apologized to the professor for my graphic design background, thinking it had too much influence on my art making. He said, "On the contrary. Use everything." I realized then that I have a sensibility that is based on a combination of instruction and inclination. My education as a graphic designer was in the Swiss/International Typographic Style. It taught me to use simplicity to convey a message. It also cemented my attraction to a particular style and helped me to use my aesthetic in other creative endeavors. By seeing what I've worked hard to build over the years, I have a clearer idea of what's behind my "gut" reaction to the new work I make.

When I'm pursuing new directions in my work, I repeatedly wonder if I'm choosing the right path. But just as often, I'm surprised by how quickly I can identify the wrong one.

One of my most useful (though scary) exercises is to show work in progress. We all know the dangers of exposing new work too early, when it's in a vulnerable stage. An audience can shut down your momentum with a negative comment, or just as bad, with a positive remark that encourages you to follow someone else's road. But if you pay attention, your reaction to their remarks can bring clarity.

In the chapter "A Hashtag Was My Muse," I described the insights that come from posting on Instagram while developing new work. One of the benefits that I did not mention was using "likes" to discover what you hate.

I was focusing on my hands as the content for a new series of images. During a visit with my elderly mother, I shot a photograph of my hand cradling hers, and posted it. The subject was an easy one to "like" and it did indeed get the most likes of any of my Instagram posts. But to me, the image was sentimental, and that is a quality that I definitely do *not* want in my photographs. The intensity of my negative reaction to my followers' approval was a great motivator. It is no small thing to be able to identify and articulate what does not work.

It's also necessary to identify our own myopia. In the chapter "Twin Art Histories," I discuss the need to be aware of our visual prejudices, and how they were formed. Let's not mistake misguided instruction for intuition.

A filmmaker friend told me how he trusts his instincts when he develops a script. He said that his intuition is a chain of decisions, and he trusts it by constantly revisiting his choices. As his work on the film progresses, he finds that what worked yesterday may need to be modified or rejected. For example, he collects mental images of friends and acquaintances, and uses aspects of their personalities for the characters in his film. But, he says, a character is her own woman, and although certain traits were right before, she has evolved, and so her persona must evolve as well. Experience has taught him that intuition—which is typically thought of as unconscious—also requires a commitment to being attentive.

My goal for my work is to venture into challenging, unknown territory. This involves courage and discomfort. I'm hoping that my accumulated arsenal of tools—training, expertise, experience, attention, and awareness—will help me to trust my instincts.

Considering Empty Space

As professionals in the arts, we learn about the "void"—more typically called "white space"—in Art 101. Whether the subject is architecture, two-dimensional art, film, dance, or theater, we know that designing the empty space is as important as designing the content that surrounds it. But it's not easy to allow emptiness. You must defend it. For those of you who are graphic designers, how many times have you argued with a client to allow those vast areas of blankness on the page? It seems, well, economically irresponsible to "waste" all that space! You have to convince your client that it is the white space that allows the content to be heard.

And you must also convince yourself. It takes confidence to allow empty space in your work. Whenever I exhibit my artwork, I feel pressure to ensure that the audience will be entertained. I want them to know that I have worked hard. I want them to see my depth and commitment. I want them to feel well-fed. So as I begin to select the material for the exhibition, I tend to include it all, to fill up the room. But as my confidence grows, I remove the extraneous and add more emptiness.

Empty space is there to allow the content to breathe. It is also there to allow the audience to participate. Jon Jerde, the well-known architect whose projects included seventy-five sites across 305 square miles for the 1984 Olympics, said it well: "The structures are expensive, but the space between them is free." Think beyond the physical structure itself and consider the human activity that its spaces encourage. In a similar way, an artist can provide the space for a viewer to bring and insert her own thoughts and experiences. Because the space is as important as the content, it must be a conscious and integral part of the design.

In my teaching, I use the idea of empty space as a metaphor. When I develop a syllabus, I also design the activities in which I will not be present. On the first day of class, I tell my students, "By the end of this course, I hope to be the least important person in this room." I believe that in addition to providing the content, my role is to create an environment that contains an active void. I need to disappear enough for my students to jump in and fill the learning environment with their own excitement and discovery. Again, as in my artwork, it takes confidence to leave that space empty.

I have a friend who teaches memoir writing. In every session, students read a short piece of their own writing. In the first two classes, my friend makes notes as she listens, and then delivers a constructive critique. In the next class, instead of delivering her critique first, she waits for the participation of the students. Inevitably, there is an awkward silence.

Initially, my friend found it hard to remain quiet. She feels that it is her job to keep the class engaged, to be imparting knowledge. In other words, as she told me, she had to make sure they are getting their money's worth. It required confidence to not fill the silence with her own critique. She had to trust that this emptiness was essential; it allowed the students to develop their own responses. When her students began to talk, there was a new energy that continued not only during the coffee breaks, but between classes as well.

Of course, empty space is not just about leaving blank spots. One has to establish content and structure to be successful in eliciting real participation, whether from a viewer or a student. One must be vigilant, constantly paying attention to the shape of the void. But that's the obvious part. The difficult part is having the confidence to hold back.

Permission to Loiter

I want to loiter. I want to show up at the station long before my train is scheduled to depart. I want to sit in the reading room of the library and not read anything. I want to spend too much time doing too little.

I've just completed a large collaborative project that culminated in an interactive, multimedia exhibition. I'd been involved with the work for over a year, much of which was spent experimenting. As with most exhibits, the month leading up to the show became increasingly more directed. During the week of on-site installation, each day had a purpose and a plan with a specified outcome.

And now I am back home. The exhibit and its opening were energizing, and I'm excited about entering this precious, unscripted phase that exists between the completion of one project and the start of another. For me, it is a period that is meant for replacing strict efficiency with lenient meandering. I'm eager to begin a new cycle—to once again be at the place in my work where I am open to surprises, where the unknowns outnumber the knowns.

I'm also nervous. I'm faced with what is essentially a huge blank canvas. What comes next? What quest will be compelling enough that I will want to devote a significant portion of my life to its pursuit? *What is the plan?*

This is a familiar feeling for many of us. We were taught to have a direction, a five-year plan that we then break down into day-by-day lists. When we fear emptiness and lack of purpose, we rush to fill the void. And before we know it, that precious, empty space has disappeared.

An artist's work cannot begin with a business plan. For me, a plan is antithetical. The most authentic endeavors—the personal projects that stick and are the most deeply engaging—are the ones that sneak up on me. I don't find them; they find me.

Loitering, by definition, means being unproductive. It is about spending (i.e., wasting) time without a specific purpose. As I reflect on the work I have produced over the past decade, I realize that each long-term project started with, essentially, loitering. A month of daily beach walks, which began with no other goal than a round trip to and from the pier, turned into a limited-edition portfolio. A year of bicoastal travel, which consisted of hours and hours spent waiting in airports and train stations, instigated an obsession with shooting surreptitious videos with my cell phone. Those video clips formed the basis of a series of etchings and a sixteen-monitor video installation. Early mornings of hanging out in cafés, where I eavesdropped on annoying cell phone conversations, was the impetus for an interactive installation of sight and sound.

In each project, it was weeks, if not months, before I realized that I was beginning a new body of work. In the earliest stages, I was collecting material—experiences, artifacts, ideas—without knowing it. And by the time I started to translate this material into work, I was already familiar with it. I was already confident that it was the right way to go, because I had faith in its natural momentum. All of these initial activities were "unproductive." And each turned into a project that would come to occupy me powerfully, from inception to completion.

I have learned to recognize my pattern. Now I want to trust it and immerse myself in the empty space that permits surprises and then unravel their possibilities. I want to go against the obvious urge to be productive and instead wait to see, out of the infinite number of possible directions, where my thoughts choose to linger.

In the previous chapter, "Considering Empty Space," I wrote about the pressure I felt to fill the space of an exhibition; in my desire to show that I had worked hard, I tended to include everything I had produced, to fill the room. But as my confidence grew, I removed the extraneous and added more emptiness.

And now, looking back at a completed body of work and looking forward to something that does not exist, I see that I am, once again, reminding myself to have the confidence to allow empty space. Only this time, it is not about allowing empty space in the exhibit; it is about allowing empty space in my life.

Please Touch (Without Touching)

Korean-born artist Lee Ufan is best known for his commanding land-art installations and sculptures made of steel and stone. But I fell in love with a small slab of clay that hung on a white wall in a gallery. It was flat and mostly empty except for the imprint of Lee's thumb pushing into its surface.

I didn't touch the art, nor did I witness its making. But when I looked at the piece, I felt it all: the speed at which his thumb had moved; the resistance of the clay; its slight warmth and later coldness; the slab's weight when he picked it up to inspect it.

I had just started using clay to create sculptures, and I had been immersed in an exploration of pressing and squishing. I assumed that I was affected by Lee's piece because I was so newly infatuated with the medium. But ever since, as I view art exhibits that range from drawing to multimedia, I have the same reaction: I'm aware of how an artwork feels without touching it. My fingers feel the sharpness of Simone Leigh's *White Teeth (for Ota Benga)*. My arm feels the flicking of paint in Jackson Pollock's *One: Number 31, 1950*. In other words, Lee's small, but distinctly physical gesture triggered a wake-up call to my sense of touch.

As visual artists, we have a finely tuned sense of sight. We value it above all other senses. But if we consider the sense of touch, we start to realize that it has an equally powerful, but often neglected, role in how we respond to art.

Think about it: Everything we see is informed by what we consciously and unconsciously recognize about touch. We look at a silk scarf, and we know that it glides smoothly across a bare arm but catches on Velcro. A raw carrot resists; a baked potato gives way. But in our contemplation of art, we typically focus on—and stop short at—the visual. Our language refers to patterns, forms, and colors. Our sense of touch in our encounters with art is undernourished and undervalued. What a loss!

There are lots of places to lay the blame for our negligence. First, we could argue that sculpture deserves tactile consideration, but not painting, photography, or other 2-D works of art. This led me to think about a camera obscura photograph by Abelardo Morell. It features an upside-down projection of the Santa Maria della Salute church on the bedroom wall in a Venetian palazzo. I saw the photograph after I had spent a summer in Venice. My room there was not in a palazzo, but its view included a portion of that church, and its furnishings were of a similar period.

I've always described the photograph with a purely visual vocabulary: the sharply focused church, a bouquet of bright pink flowers, ornate frames around pictures and mirrors. Now when I look at the image, I imagine the feel of its contents: The hard terrazzo floor is cool to the feet on a hot and humid day; the dresser drawers scrape when they are pulled open; the frames are heavy and accumulate grime in their crevices.

We could also blame our contemporary society and culture. All day long, we navigate our lives with our fingertips tapping and sliding over glass. You may have seen the diagram called a cortical homunculus. It explains the areas of our bodies' greatest sensitivity using exaggerated depictions of parts of the human figure. For example, the hands are huge compared with the torso and legs. It's ironic: Our magnificent capacity to discern our world through our fingers has been relegated to a slick surface of nothingness.

And of course, museums and galleries don't allow us to touch the art. The reasons are obvious and sensible: Physical contact threatens the works' longevity and preservation. But it's enlightening to note the history of museums, and visitors' urge, and even expectation, to handle items. In her book *The Deepest Sense: A Cultural History of Touch*, Constance Classen discusses the sense of touch from diverse perspectives, including religion, sex, war, and medicine. In the section "Touch in the Museum," she writes, "In 1786, German traveler Sophie von La Roche wrote of her visit to the British Museum 'Nor could I restrain my desire to touch the ashes of an urn on which a female figure was being mourned. I felt it gently, with great feeling. . . . I pressed the grain of dust between my fingers tenderly, just as her best friend might have once grasped her hand.'"

Later in the book, Classen quotes the 18th-century philosopher Denis Diderot: "Of all the senses the eye [is] the most superficial . . . [and] touch the most profound and the most philosophical."

The next time you look at art, try to see what it feels like.

I
See
What
You're
Saying

Last week, I put on a jacket I hadn't worn for a year, and when I reached into the pocket, I felt a small, unfamiliar object. A couple of seconds went by before I realized what it was: a crumpled up, hardened packet of sugar. Normally, the moment would have passed as quickly as it had come, but instead, I touched the packet again, recollecting a passage I had just read: "We see with our brains, not with our eyes."

Thinking about the fertile landscapes that exist in the mind's eye, I began to wonder: How do our brains process the visual environment around us? A friend suggested the book *The Brain That Changes Itself* by Norman Doidge, which relates wide-ranging scientific research through interviews and case histories—a very readable book for a neophyte like myself. As soon as I got into the first chapter, random mundane occurrences became relevant.

After my re-acquaintance with the crumpled sugar packet, I read Doidge's interview with Paul Bach-y-Rita, a neuroscientist noted for his work in neuroplasticity. "When a blind man uses a cane," Bach-y-Rita says, "he sweeps it back and forth. . . . Though his hand sensors are where he gets the information and where the cane 'interfaces' with him, what he subjectively perceives is . . . the layout of the room: chairs, walls, feet, the three-dimensional space."

Bach-y-Rita determined that skin and its touch receptors could substitute for a retina. When I felt the object in my pocket, I "saw" that it was a sugar packet because my fingers (i.e., receptors) gave me the information to perceive its shape, size, contour, and crunchiness.

I happened upon a Public Broadcasting Service (PBS) documentary about an art school. One of the teachers emphasized the importance of simple observation, stating that her best students spent twenty minutes just looking at the model before they touched a pencil. Later, I read Doidge's example of how the brain can "recruit other operators," vastly increasing its processing power, provided there is a roadblock between the operator and its usual function: "Someone presented with an overwhelming task, such as memorizing *The Iliad*, might blindfold himself [and listen to it instead] in order to recruit the operators usually devoted to sight." This made me wonder: What if I could use my ears to see? I imagined a strange scenario: a life drawing class where, instead of looking at the model for those twenty minutes, you closed your eyes and listened as he described himself verbally.

Recently, in the middle of a project that required a lot of research, I had to leave town for a couple of weeks. There was no way I could carry all the books I was using, so I ordered some of them for my Kindle. But when I reached my destination and tried to resume my work, I encountered a problem. I had thought that I could easily search for the sections of text I had previously noted by using key words. Instead, I realized that my recollection of where those sections were had less to do with words, and more to do with perceptual clues like spatial relationships, shapes, and how the weight of the book felt in my hands.

I could "see," for example, a favorite quote. It was at the top of a left-hand page. I had underlined it and scribbled a note sideways in the margin. The book was heavy and thick, and I knew that the passage was in the first third of the book, because I remembered that there was a lot more of the book's volume in my right hand than in my left. How ironic: I had brought my Kindle to avoid carrying so many pounds of books and then found that I missed holding their weight.

I have always believed that each of my senses provided a separate and distinct way of feeding me information. But I'm beginning to understand that my brain is not so single-minded. Instead, its "operators" work together, processing incoming information in the most splendid manner. I have a favorite tree, and now when I look at it, I realize that its beauty lies not only in its appearance, but in the numerous ways I perceive it: its rough bark, the sound and movement of its leaves when the wind starts blowing, and even the feeling of that wind on my face.

Pursuing Your Mind's Eye

At the Museum of the City of New York, a video by the artist Neil Goldberg featured short close-ups of individuals identifying the Manhattan street corner where they are standing. As I watched the video, I realized that the images I was really "seeing" were in my head. Fourteenth and Tenth? I pictured the High Line. Eighty-Ninth and Fifth? The Guggenheim. Simultaneously, I saw my own memories: climbing the stairs to the High Line, waiting for a friend in the Guggenheim rotunda. And then my thoughts went farther afield, calling up hazy images for my own creative work.

I'm usually not so cognizant of what I see in my mind's eye. But I became obsessed with the subject as I developed my exhibit for the Rhode Island School of Design (RISD) Museum. Over several months, I asked friends and acquaintances to use the Photo Booth app to record themselves while they worked on their laptops in their favorite café or library. In their videos, they occasionally pause and enter a deep-thought space, gazing away from, or beyond, their computer screen. I saw this again and again, and it made me wonder: *What are they looking at?*

When I asked my "subjects" what they had been working on, they remembered easily: designing a book proposal, puzzling out the script for a play, conceiving characters for a novel. But when I asked what they had been seeing in their mind's eye, they were stumped. They acknowledged that whatever they were imagining was essential to conceptualizing their ideas, and yet they could not articulate—let alone recall—what they "saw."

As creative professionals, we mine the imagery of our physical world; our brains absorb massive amounts of visual data. Our mind's eye is filled with animated scenarios that summon our emotions, senses, and experiences. We use them to find design solutions and create original ideas. But do we access these scenes as robustly as we could? If we paid closer attention to our mind's eye, would we be better at pushing our creative boundaries?

In his book *The Mind's Eye*, the neurologist Oliver Sacks explores "mental images of an . . . abstract and visionary kind, images which have never been seen by the physical eye, but which can be conjured up by the creative imagination."

Sacks recounts the experiences of people who are blind—some from birth, some at an early age, others later in life—and the ways in which their visual capacity has grown, despite—or because of—their loss. He describes Zoltan Torey, a man who became blind at age twenty-one. Determined to utilize his "inner eye," Torey "developed a remarkable power of generating, holding, and manipulating images in his mind."

Sacks continues, " . . . his newly strengthened visual imagery enabled him to think in ways that had not been available to him before, allowed him to project himself inside machines and other systems, to envisage systems, models and designs. . . . He became able to imagine, to visualize the inside of a differential gearbox in action as if from inside its casing."

Reflecting on these anecdotes, I thought: Do we need to experience loss in order to gain an ability? Or is the capacity already there, waiting for us to find it by being more attentive?

Perhaps you've heard stories of scientists like Einstein and Faraday, whose inner visions led to groundbreaking discoveries. Thomas West, in his 1997 book *In the Mind's Eye*, cites the German chemist August Kekulé, who came upon the structure of the benzene ring, and subsequently revolutionized organic chemistry. Kekulé wrote: "I turned the chair to the fireplace and fell into a half sleep. The atoms flitted before my eyes. Long rows, variously, more closely, united; all in movement wriggling and turning like snakes. . . . One of the snakes seized its own tail, and the image whirled before my eyes." He goes on to describe waking and working on his hypothesis, ending with, "Let us learn to dream."

As I mentioned earlier, my "video subjects" had difficulty depicting what they had seen in their mind's eye. But one woman, a painter, thought further and wrote, "I see the future; little hypotheticals playing out, developing and growing, turning from movie clips into abstraction. Sometimes, on the train, staring at the hem of a dress or a polished watch face, the reality before my eyes disappears, and I see only the abstraction of my thoughts." She added that this attention made her think of her paintings differently. By being more aware, she gained insight.

If we are lucky, our mind's eye is well developed, and it offers us a constant rush of vivid imagery. Perhaps we don't need to learn to dream; we just need to strengthen our grasp.

Listening Like a Singer

Normally I turn on the radio in the morning. But sometimes I want to keep the early hours separate from the outside world. So instead, I sing.

I repeat the same few songs. My favorite is Joni Mitchell's "Urge for Going," about the coming of winter. Pretending that I'm performing, I concentrate on mimicking the melancholy way that she bends the note on choice words. There's another version by Tom Rush. He sings that note straight. For me, the bent note (or lack of it) affects the whole mood of the song. I doubt I would have noticed this tiny but defining detail if I had not been singing the song so diligently.

In other words, my awareness deepened when I shifted my perspective—from being a passive listener to listening as though I were a singer.

One of my most heavily dog-eared books is *Reading Like a Writer*, by Francine Prose. Its premise is that one of the best ways to educate oneself as a writer is to read very closely. (A sample of the table of contents says a lot about her methodology: Chapter Two: Words; Chapter Three: Sentences; Chapter Four: Paragraphs.) Prose wants readers to apply something specific from what they are reading—like a bold first line from a novel or a taut description from a short story—to help them in their own writing. She cites a time when she was struggling to compose a party scene, and states that James Joyce's "The Dead" taught her "how to orchestrate the voices of the party guests into a chorus from which the principal players step forward. . . "

Her book is useful to me as a writer. But this type of close reading of any medium can teach me a lot about developing my own work, no matter the medium. I'm not (nor will I ever be) a singer. But by listening as though I were a performer of Joni Mitchell's song, I was hyper-aware of how a detail can shape a mood. My concentration on a single note became a technique that serves other areas. For example, during a video project, I was editing a series of short, minute-long clips, and I was not happy with the feeling they conveyed. Then I recalled Joni's bended note: She had gently forced the listener to linger in that moment. I tried holding for an extra two seconds at the end of each clip. Those two seconds made the other sixty work.

In one of my classes, students from diverse disciplines were collaborating to develop an exhibition of multimedia portraits. We wanted to make sure that the portraits were distinct but also unified.

I had seen an interview with Stephen Daldry, the director of the film *The Hours*, based on Michael Cunningham's novel of the same name. It follows the stories of Virginia Woolf and two women of later generations who were influenced by her novel *Mrs. Dalloway*. Daldry said that his biggest challenge was to make sure that the actors "were all part of the same production." This was tough because the film repeatedly cuts back and forth between the three women's stories. Daldry described one of his solutions: "A lot of the emotion in [Meryl Streep's] scene is expressed through breaking eggs, this very rhythmic action of cracking and separating eggs . . . in the back of my head I sort of knew that later down the line I'd probably be using eggs in [a] Virginia Woolf [scene] and keep the idea of food in some way . . . in the different periods."

I found the movie and watched it with my students, focusing on the goal of making all the portraits ("actors") exist together as part of the same exhibition ("production"). Paying attention to the food scenes that Daldry had referred to, we looked for the similarities in how the characters were simultaneously distinct and similar. We decided to create an accompanying catalogue of all the portraits, featuring each of the participant's eyes. In this way, all the various "actors"— i.e., participants and mediums—existed separately, but always had a single, unified reference: the eyes.

In a collaboration with the choreographer Martha Mason, we engaged in a dialogue in which we familiarized ourselves with each other's medium. When I shoot photographs, I'm typically looking for discreet single moments; a dancer's work is about creating a flow of transitions. As a result of seeing through our respective filters, Martha became aware of constructing moments of stillness, and I began to follow the flow of action in between.

Are there disciplines outside your own that might help you see your work in a new light? There's a freedom and openness that comes with dipping into a new practice. Especially when you make it part of your own.

Creative Ratios

It takes Jerry Seinfeld a long time to develop a joke. After he writes many drafts on a yellow pad, he tries the result on a live audience, attuned to any point where their attention strays. Then he reworks it. In a *New York Times* video describing the development of a single sentence for a joke about Pop-Tarts, he says, "So now I'm looking for the connective tissue that gives me the really tight, smooth link . . . and if it's just a split second too long, you will shave letters off of words, you will count syllables. . ."

All that work, one little line.

Think about the time you spend reading a poem or standing in front of a painting in a gallery. An artwork that took months or years to create is typically looked at or listened to (or tasted!) for less than a few minutes.

In other words, the ratio of time spent by an artist to build skills and create work to the time the finished piece is viewed or experienced is daunting.

Such is the nature of the way we experience art; the encounter is not a long one. This can feel particularly painful when we consider our own work. I find it tough when I have an exhibit and I see how briefly the work is viewed and how short a time it's being shown, compared to the amount of time it took to develop.

If I ended here, it would be a depressing conclusion. But as I picture the paintings and sculptures and choreography that I love, it occurs to me that the concept of the creative ratio can exist in a more positive, fruitful realm.

Powerful art stays in your memory, your mind's eye, your psyche. It endures long after the actual viewing, even when that viewing is a matter of minutes. Vija Celmins, a painter, printmaker, and sculptor, is one of my favorite artists. I'm attracted to both her process and her subject matter, especially her interest in the surface of the ocean, from her early drawings, like *Sea Drawing with Whale*, circa 1969, to her later lithographs, woodcuts, and mezzotint prints, like *Untitled (Ocean Mezzotint)*, 2016. Even though I've only seen her drawings and prints briefly, I can envision them clearly; Celmins's process—her slow and steady progression, her mastery of different mediums, her commitment to conceptual investigation—has made a deep impact that stays. I keep on getting what she has given.

All the work you did for that one script, that single poster, or that short poem is in your data bank. Everything you tried but discarded is valuable. What a waste it would be if you forgot about the pieces of the process that led to the product! I've taught a class for years where I ask students to look back at their past work—the material that's collecting dust on a shelf or buried on their hard drives—and lay it all out. Inevitably, they see connections that suggest a direction. They are surprised to see how much endures. An abundance of old ideas is waiting to bring insight to new work.

I have a friend who was a professional dancer. On a recent visit, she paused as she entered her living room. She said, "I love the feeling of moving from one room to another." It's not just the physical sensation. It's also the pleasing awareness of her body in relationship to its surroundings: the curve and the straight, the hard and soft, the hide and reveal. Though she no longer dances, she carries her years of training, choreography, and technique with her in the simplest, shortest moments.

It's easy to get distracted by a desire for volume and to measure the success of work by our productivity and exposure. We mistakenly assume that the best work-to-results ratio is one where "quantity in" is equal to "quantity out." But I think Vija Celmins had it right when she said: "My favorite thing would be to have a show, then take it down and paint it again. Then show it again, then take it down and paint it again just to readjust it a tiny bit. My wish would be to work on one painting for the rest of my life."

Sewing
101

When I signed up for the class "Sewing 101," my goals were practical and immediate. I had been working with plaster for four years, making sculptures that involved digging and scraping and carrying heavy blocks. I wanted to use lighter materials and make objects that had fluidity and movement. I decided to learn how to work with fabric.

What was intended as a quick study for a few skills instead seeped into daily thoughts and activities, sneaking up on me when I didn't expect it. I found myself initiating conversations with strangers, asking, for example, "Did you sew the lacy cuffs onto your jacket sleeves?" This led to longer discussions that were thoughtful, whimsical, and sometimes emotional. Sewing, a subject that had previously occupied no space in my consciousness, was giving me insights about the way we live.

On the first day of class, I learned the basics of using a sewing machine. I hadn't touched one since I was a teenager, and, although today's sewing machines have a slew of software, the analog basics are still there. Threading the bobbin, running the thread through the needle, lowering the presser foot—it was just like my mom's old Singer.

Later that day, back in my usual world of technology, I noticed that my computer was acting funny. While I was typing, random words would suddenly select and highlight themselves. Worse, I was halfway through composing an email, and it sent itself. I brought my laptop to the Apple store. The diagnosis: a faulty track pad. The salesperson ordered a new one, and three anxious days later, I retrieved my computer. Now I have a track pad that obeys my demands instead of its own.

Normally, I would consider this a relief and a victory: problem solved. Instead, I'm annoyed. With the sewing machine, if something goes wrong, I understand why. When the thread gets tangled or material bunches up, the reasons are clear. The mechanics are obvious and analog. Yes, I'm comparing Apples to oranges, so to speak. But my track pad incident reminded me that the ways my most essential tools work (and break) are beyond my comprehension.

When my brother was in the hospital for long periods of cancer treatment, he was almost always cold. He had a down parka, but it was awkward and inconvenient when the port in his chest needed to be accessed. I looked online for clothing that would accommodate his particular needs, but there was nothing that addressed all the aspects. So I bought a sweatshirt that was soft and warm, in his favorite color, and I devised a design. I cut the material to create new openings, and hand stitched a row of snaps. The result was acceptable, and it felt good to see him wearing it.

Now, years later, I remember the positive act of sewing itself. The calm monotony of stitching kept my hands busy during my visits. And I liked making the pieces of a 3-D puzzle come together.

Perhaps most important, sewing a sweatshirt was a task I could control. I could not cure my brother; I could not make the research go faster; I could not buy him more time. I could not control his disease, but I could control fabric and thread.

When I told people I was taking a sewing class, many responded with nostalgia. "I have six siblings, and my mom sewed a lot." "I remember my mother repairing hand-me-downs or making Halloween costumes." Then the discussion turned to our society's proclivity for consumption rather than conservation. "Clothes are cheap, and so is the fabric. When your shirt rips, you throw it away and buy a new one."

One of my favorite artists is Andrea Zittel. I first heard about her in 1991, when she began designing and sewing a single outfit for each season. These *Personal Uniforms* were a response to her frustration with our society's mandate that we wear a different outfit every day—evidence of our consumerist culture. I mentioned Zittel to a friend, and she suggested that instead of a single uniform, we consider a template: Take a few basic, well-constructed garments, and upgrade them by adding utilitarian but playful variations, like a pocket for a phone, or loops for keys and glasses.

Sewing stores are great places for inspiring change. I spent an hour in one store, where I must have touched (or, more accurately, fondled) two dozen different fabrics—velvet, silk, flannel, tulle. . . . Each bolt promised the creative freedom that comes with using new materials. It was an invitation to push boundaries and occupy new territories, both literal and imagined. I have an idea for a soft, colorful, whimsical sculpture. It's time for a new exploration.

A Line Goes for a Walk

After I completed my Sewing 101 class, I went to FABSCRAP, a nonprofit that recycles excess fabric from textile industry users. FABSCRAP's warehouse, which is located in the Brooklyn Army Terminal, also sells fabric—by the pound! When I arrived, I was directed to an area filled with large bins and bolts: silks, suedes, cottons; thick, thin, shiny, matte. I loaded yards of assorted colors onto the counter, feeling giddy, like a speed-shopping contestant on a TV game show. I stopped at eight pounds (forty bucks), squeezed it all into my backpack, and went straight to my studio.

FYI, I'm on a mission. My artwork has been black and white (and, frankly, somber) for years, and it's time for a change. My venture into color and cloth is a quest for lightening up in my work. Playfulness—doing solely for the sake of doing—has been absent for too long, and I want it back.

As soon as I got to my studio, I tacked up the swaths of fabric. No hesitation, no thought about placement; just grab and tack, grab and tack. In minutes, the wall was singing—royal blue, emerald green, mustard yellow, hot pink—fourteen colors altogether.

I cut two ten-by-ten-inch squares—one red, one orange—and sat down at my new sewing machine. I stitched the pieces together, letting the machine guide me on a random, meandering route. I thought of Paul Klee's famous proclamation: "A drawing is simply a line going for a walk." I stuffed the blob shape with shredded scraps. It was squishy and goofy and unexpectedly adorable.

Then, after an hour of joyful, lighthearted fun. . . . THUD! The left side of my brain slammed on the brakes. It took over and demanded answers: What is the goal? Where is this going? WHAT'S THE PLAN?

Damn! How can I keep playing when logic is muscling in?

I went home and searched my bookshelves for Klee's *Pedagogical Sketchbook*, hoping to find the quote that would justify my playtime. There, on page 16, was an illustration: a simple black stroke with the caption "An active line on a walk, moving freely, without goal. A walk for a walk's sake." At first, I felt vindicated, and promised myself I would return to my state of play. But I kept reading. That first drawing was Figure 1 in Exercise 1 in a primer of forty-three exercises for Bauhaus students. Klee's text was carefully articulated, specific, and methodical. A walk, while appreciated for its own sake, was the first step of a progression, one leading to the next, each based on observation.

Later that week, I told a friend about my nagging left brain/ right brain headache. She is Korean, and English is her second language; she chooses her words carefully. She said, "It's important to interrogate your work." I'm a fan of self-reflection, but the word "interrogate" implied a tougher, more challenging effort.

Back in the studio, I decided to interrogate each period of play. I toggled between the two sides: First, I immersed myself in a goal-free activity, then I used the discipline of note-taking to investigate it. What did I learn? How did it inform my work?

Here are my observations so far.

The speed at which I can work with color is exhilarating, marrying one solid hue to another, and another. The material is cheap and plentiful. It's physical in exactly the way I need: light, soft, and pliable. All of this tells me to put away the heavy plaster from my last body of work and relieve some of the heaviness of illness and loss.

Stretchy spandex is funny. Silk is slippery and voluminous. Transparent fabric is, well, transparent. These qualities present metaphors to explore—and I do love metaphors!

Stuffing these sewn blobs makes them come alive. When I use minuscule beads, the shapes squiggle like they're dancing. Discarded scraps make good filling for weird contours. Lined up, these little figures are an anthropomorphic army. They make me feel silly, comfy, and defiant.

In the previous chapter, I mentioned the idea of clothing as templates that could be added onto, with colorful pockets for phones and loops for keys. The idea of practical additions has now been replaced by puffy characters that are proliferating and attaching to whatever outfit or furniture they're attracted to. It makes sitting down a contact sport.

I know I will arrive at a point where goal-free activities will be replaced by a specific direction. But for now, I'm exploring, and yes, it's fun. Examination and instinct can go hand in hand. As Sibyl Moholy-Nagy says of Klee in her introduction to *Pedagogical Sketchbook*, "Exactitude winged by intuition was the goal he held out for his students."

You're Already Working

During a long and troubling time in southern California, I developed a routine to counteract my unsteady moods. Each day, I walked along the beach for a mile to the pier, a huge symmetrical structure that loomed above me. I stood at the end between its columns, until I felt centered.

When the tide was low, the water was far away, and the sand was dry. At high tide, waves came up to my ankles. One morning, I brought along my new camera, adding to my practice: Walk to the pier, center myself, and shoot from the same spot. Each photograph was a record, not only of the view, but also of the date and time I had shot it. I downloaded a tide chart and paired each photo's time with the corresponding tide: 10:24 a.m., tide .57 feet rising. 12:36 p.m., tide 3.98 feet falling. 7:48 a.m., tide 1.91 feet rising. Up, down, up. It read like a diary of my moods.

During those months, I thought I had not been making any art. But I was wrong. I was already deep into a body of work without knowing it. The photographs, along with text records of the tides and phrases from my journal, eventually became a fourteen-print portfolio of photographs with accompanying letterpress text.

It's often only in hindsight that we, as artists, can identify the invisible but crucial period of gestation. You may not consciously know it, but this is an integral part of your practice. You are already working.

When I first moved to New York, I experienced the classic love/hate relationship with the city. The overwhelming barrage of sights and sounds both repelled and attracted me. I was especially drawn to the mundane and revealing cell phone conversations, and I got into the habit of eavesdropping and jotting down phrases. Then I read a quote by John Cage: "Wherever we are, what we hear is mostly noise. When we ignore it, it disturbs us. When we listen to it, we find it fascinating." His quote showed me that my routine of collecting these fragments was not frivolous. I had been working. What started as bits of an urban soundscape became the content of a multimedia installation.

During a summer in Maine, I bicycled early each morning along the rocky seashore of Acadia National Park. Tourists came and went, often leaving behind a plethora of rock "sculptures." One day, feeling mischievous, I got off my bike and knocked a few piles down. I did it again the next day, and the next. I set my camera on a tripod and shot short videos of my escapades. One morning in August, I saw a National Park Service Ranger get out of her truck, survey the scene, and kick over a cluster. She told me that these structures were a blight, overrunning the park's natural environment. After that conversation, I realized that I had been setting up my camera to capture the beauty of the landscape, which was revealed only after I swept the rock piles away. As with previous projects, what I had considered to be a fleeting diversion was the basis for new work—an installation of over eighty short videos playing on thirteen discarded, heavy, ancient TVs.

I'm no fan of war paraphernalia, so the Arms and Armor Department at the New York Metropolitan Museum was never on my go-to list. But one day, instead of running through on my way to the café, I stopped to look at a display of cuirassier armor made in Italy between 1610 and 1630. How could I not marvel at its exquisite craftsmanship? A small indentation in the chest area drew my attention. The museum label described this easily overlooked detail: "Before an armor of this type was finished," the text stated, "it was fired at with a pistol to test its effectiveness against bullets, and the bullet dents [known as 'proof marks'] were left as a guarantee of the strength and quality of its steel."

That armor was a metaphor for the protection I was seeking for my brother, who was ill and receiving experimental treatments. Protection meant effort, skill, optimism, and hope. The trips to the museum were the beginning of a sculpture series, even though none of what I saw or made found its way into my final work. The original impetus—the determination to heal and be healed—remained throughout.

Think back to an artwork that you completed. Now think further back—before you were consciously making that art—to an activity or curiosity that seemed like a passing distraction, but stuck with you, refusing to disappear. Was that so-called distraction actually the work's foundation? You were already working.

3
PROTECTION

*A creative practice provides a foundation
when we encounter life's painful realities—
in particular, losing people we love.
We can't predict how difficult times will
affect or alter our lives. But as artists,
we can call upon our well-honed practice
to allow grief to reside in our creative work.*

Between
Data
and
Emotion

In your lifetime, you will have a personal relationship with cancer. You may be a patient yourself, or you will know someone—a relative, partner, or friend—who is sick. In November 2014, my brother was diagnosed with a rare blood cancer. His immediate reaction to this news was to educate himself, to gain knowledge through every source available. I joined him as his "co-CEO" in research. I have no background in medicine, and my studies in science stopped in tenth grade, but somehow, motivated by a combination of love and a high-speed internet connection, I learned to converse in the foreign language of cancer, using terms like "cytogenetics", "RVD therapy", and "allogeneic stem cell transplant." When I read a clinical report and came across an incomprehensible phrase, I was like a dog with a bone.

As members of the 21st-century world of medicine, we are a population of caregivers and care-seekers that is accustomed to researching whatever we choose. We have access to resources that explain the minute details of a disease as well as the latest advances in its treatment. This is empowering, but it is also daunting. There's a deluge of data, both from the supporting resources (the internet, oncologists, cancer foundations, support groups, and clinics) and from the patient (X-rays, MRIs, PET scans, blood tests, and biopsies).

On top of that, the data is dynamic: The research is continually presenting new facts and figures, and so is the patient. The numbers are in constant flux, potentially steering life-or-death decisions.

The more information I collected for and about my brother, the more I felt the need to harness it. How do I, as his "co-CEO," deal with the overwhelming volume of evolving data?

I called a very smart colleague who knows a lot about information design, and, more importantly, about me. I asked him for examples of software that would help me to comprehend, organize, and track this explosion of material. He started to describe the workspace program Evernote and then stopped. He asked, "Are you approaching this problem as a researcher or as a sister?" His question was pivotal for me. He made me see that I had considered only half of the design problem. By focusing just on the scientific data, I had neglected the onslaught of feelings that accompanies each new discovery. In other words, I had left out the emotions. I needed a system that would help me to comprehend my dual role as researcher and family member—a way to deal with data that was necessary to learn, but also painful to absorb.

Knowing that my approach to understanding most things is by interacting with them physically, my colleague suggested that I set aside a space where the array of content could live: a place where I could stack it up or spread it out, but where I could also "close the door"—both literally and metaphorically—when I needed to. When we hung up, I felt relieved, calmer, but with a sense of renewed energy.

Later that evening, I poured myself a glass of wine and walked around my apartment, opening each closet. One was filled with a disorganized jumble of clothes, books, and folders, most of which had not been touched for years. I woke up early the next morning and spent most of that Saturday emptying the closet. I piled up ancient and useless files, dragged them to the recycling bin, and then arranged to have the file cabinet hauled away. I tore out ugly plastic wire shelving and spackled the holes. I created a space that was pristine and white, ready for whatever it needed to contain.

On Sunday, I decided to look at the material that I had accumulated since my brother's diagnosis. The bulk of it lives within the more than five hundred emails that I've received. My plan was to quickly review my inboxes to make sure that I had kept important records. But I ended up reading every email, allowing myself to remember the impact of each one before moving on. As I went through them, I copied their subject headings—"FW: Targeted T cell therapy," "Re: Pain management team," and "Great news: Light chains are normal!"—and pasted each line, in chronological order, into a spreadsheet. Then I printed out all the pages and put them in a three-ring binder and placed it on the floor of the closet.

A friend who was familiar with my role came over to help me "interact" with the data. We approached the inside of the closet as a cocoon-like canvas. We traced delicate outlines of each other's bodies on the walls and drew vague diagrams and calendars, allowing ourselves a respite from the hard facts. After my friend left, I shut the closet door.

When we engage with another's illness, we occupy the dual roles of researcher and loved one. We are constantly trying to balance a seesaw. One side holds the scientific data, the other, our emotions. We need tools to deal with the heavy weight of both.

A Hashtag Was My Muse

In the previous chapter, I wrote about my brother's cancer and my struggle to absorb my dual role as researcher and caregiver. I described my decision to empty out a closet in my apartment, creating a place that could hold the medical information I had collected and printed, but could also hold my emotions. That closet became the designated space where I would transform data and emotion into a new body of creative work. I had no idea what that would be.

These drawings, along with the charts and notebooks full of data, showed potential. These nebulous images and piles of paper waited for me to take the next step.

But I froze. The marks that we made with lightness suddenly held too much meaning. They became too precious to touch or alter, adding to the burden I was already carrying around. The original impulse, which was to make a fluid, creative space, was instead being weighed down by the obligation to become something.

Some artists and writers are afraid of the empty canvas or the blank page. It's not the emptiness that scares me; it's the page that has a promising first sentence, or the paper with the graceful first mark. Yes, my initial spark was good. But what is my next mark? What is my next sentence? As soon as I give these explorations the responsibility of becoming a finished piece, I start to hold back.

Luckily, I stumbled upon an antidote to my cautious behavior: #The100DayProject, the brainchild of Elle Luna. It's based on Michael Bierut's now-classic workshop at Yale in which he instructed his design students to choose one action and repeat it every day for one hundred days.

Anyone could join in. Participants were instructed to decide on an action and post it daily on Instagram with the hashtag #the100DayProject, along with a related hashtag of their own, i.e., #100Daysof________.

I opened the door of my closet. There was an outline of my friend's left hand, and I chose my hashtag: #100DaysofLeftHands. I made a commitment to a creative study of nothing more than left hands. The only thing I was obliged to complete was one hundred days of Instagram posts.

Sometimes, I gave a lot of attention to images, like my sketches of the left hand of the model in my Friday open drawing class. Other times, I used my phone to capture whatever caught my eye during the day (or at 11:45 at night, just before deadline!).

I posted images and printed them out, pasting them onto the closet's walls.

After a few weeks, I realized that my posts and printouts were a journal, and many of my drawings or photographs had a connection to my brother's illness. Some were overt: blue surgical gloves in the drugstore, my hand holding a thick caregiver's manual, a snapshot of the TV screen of a surgeon's hand in the documentary *Cancer: The Emperor of All Maladies*. Others were more subtle: a friend's fingers cradling mine, a ragged hole in a worn leather glove, my hand gripping a canoe paddle during one glorious day on a lake.

I received comments on my posts that deepened the project. One follower initiated a repartee of hand shadows; another picked up on the medical images and wrote, "Are you OK?"

Many participants used #the100DayProject to build a pre-determined, cohesive body of work. Each post was a single fully realized piece that was part of a visually consistent collection. As

I followed the progression of various artists, it was like encountering beautiful seashells—each one perfectly formed, and, when placed side by side, an impressive set of finalized work, ready for public appreciation.

My drawings, photographs, and notes were nowhere near finished art, but #100DaysofLeftHands became a committed exploration: a stable and comfortable way to nourish the early seeds of a vulnerable new body of work. By removing the severe prescription for completion, I knew that I had, at least, taken the next step.

What
a
Poem
Holds

In her poem *The Gate*, Marie Howe writes about her brother, who died when he was twenty-eight years old. The poem has stayed with me, in particular the last five lines:

> *This is what you have been waiting for, he used to say to me.*
> *And I'd say, What?*
>
> *And he'd say, This—holding up my cheese and mustard*
> *sandwich.*
> *And I'd say, What?*
>
> *And he'd say, This, sort of looking around.*

There are a handful of poems that have accompanied the changes in my life. Each one has layers of meaning that pile up and morph accordingly. How can a few simple phrases strung together affect me so personally, and over such long periods of time?

During my summer vacations in Maine, I walk to the seawall to catch the sunrise. I usually stay just a few minutes, and then I go back home, ready to move on with the day. But one summer, I found myself repeating those lines from Howe's poem, and I lingered. If it was foggy, I listened to the foghorn from the nearby lighthouse. If it was clear, I watched the lobster boats on their way to work. I looked out at the ocean and said to myself, "This is what I have been waiting for."

On a windy morning, I saw a man standing on the boulders. He was almost motionless, reeling in a kite, pulling the twine slowly and evenly. The kite pulled back, veering left and right. "No!" it said, refusing to return to land. The man was gentle but deliberate and kept reeling, and the kite kept resisting. I was afraid it was going to get shredded on the rocks. But then, just a foot or so above the ground, the kite shuddered, nodded "Yes," and lay down. The man folded it into a small, neat square, put it in a pouch, and got on his bike.

Walking home, I thought about the kite's resistance and acceptance, and I realized that the poem held another meaning for me. Early that June, my mom passed away. What I had been waiting for was the end of a very long life—one that, after tenaciously holding onto freedom, came reluctantly but gracefully to its end.

In his book *Why Poetry*, Matthew Zapruder describes a poem as "making meaning by failing to fully make meaning." Poetry—at least the poetry that I am attracted to—challenges me to make up for its vagueness; it urges me to supply my own specifics and make my own meaning. Instead of imposing an interpretation of a situation or feeling, a poem can be an empty room that holds space for whatever I need to fill it with.

The best explanation I've found of this morphing of meaning is itself a poem. *One Train May Hide Another (sign at a railroad crossing in Kenya)* by Kenneth Koch begins:

> *In a poem, one line may hide another line,*
> *As at a crossing, one train may hide another train.*

The entire poem consists of examples of single things—one love, one dream, one memory, one injustice—that hide other things.

> *One wish may hide another. And one person's reputation*
> *may hide*

*The reputation of another. One dog may conceal another
On a lawn, so if you escape the first one you're not
necessarily safe. . .*

*. . . In love, one reproach may hide another,
One small complaint may hide a great one.*

Think about your own life. Were there paths that you saw when you faced in one direction? And later, when you turned around, you found the others?

Or perhaps you have read (and copied and re-read, as I have) Mary Oliver's famous poem *Wild Geese*.

*You do not have to be good.
You do not have to walk on your knees
for a hundred miles through the desert repenting.
You only have to let the soft animal of your body
love what it loves.*

A Conversation on the Art of Protection

Making art includes terrific periods of immersion, where you focus intensely on your work. But this can also create blinders, causing your vision to become narrow and restricted to your own ideas and experience. When I feel this tendency coming on, I look for outside perspectives.

My recent body of work, titled *Like the Back of My Hand*, is about the contradictions of the body: a miraculous, self-healing machine that has an equally powerful capacity to wreak havoc on itself. In the early stages of this project, I studied different examples of protection, from the literal, like advances in immunology, to the metaphorical, like mythical figures in medieval armor. The broader the range of resources, the more my art was enriched.

So when a friend asked me to put together a panel for Brooklyn's ArtSlope festival, I saw an opportunity. What if I could assemble professionals whose work addressed the same subject— our need to protect ourselves, and our desire to protect others—but from different points of view? What a great way to expand my perceptions and knowledge! Selfish, yes, but I felt we would all gain from the exchange.

I titled the panel "Body Armor: A Conversation on the Art of Protection." I found four experts whose work responds to the body's strength and fragility in diverse disciplines: tattoo artistry, medical science, fashion design, and photography.

The tattoo artist David Sena has many devotees—especially people who find protection in metaphors. David showed us a stunning array of protective iconography: gods, dragons, evil eyes, writhing snakes, and chrysanthemums, sometimes covering the full body. Getting tattooed is a commitment to a long, painful procedure and a permanent adornment. That, in itself, is proof of strength.

Diane Felsen is a scientist who views the body as a different kind of canvas: She researches skin cancer and the immune system. Diane describes our skin as armor: It serves as a protective barrier for infection control, and it provides crucial sensing for hot and cold, touch and pressure. But if damaged, our skin can turn against us, generating abnormal cell proliferation and tumors.

Lucy Jones's creations provide physical and psychological protection. She designs clothing for people with disabilities, marrying style and function by altering mainstream fashion's design process. In her project *Seated Design*, Lucy modified patterns to accommodate the needs of people who are confined to wheelchairs. The beauty of the garment is a vital attribute of the clothing.

Peter Angelo Simon is a prolific photographer. Peter chronicled Muhammad Ali at his training camp in Pennsylvania as he prepared to reclaim the title of boxing heavyweight champion of the world, and the resulting images were published in Peter's book, *Muhammad Ali: Fighter's Heaven 1974*. In addition to physical preparation, the camp was designed to nourish Ali's image of himself as a champion. In other words, Ali was developing both his physical and mental armor.

After the panelists' presentations, the discussion was ripe with connections. For example, Lucy recalled two conversations she had had with people she was designing for. One was with a war veteran who tattooed his prosthesis because he didn't want to look like a medical model. The other was with a woman who had a skin disorder and tattooed the adjacent skin to match her ailment. It occurred to me that choosing to be unique rather than trying to be "normal" might be the best form of protection.

I went home that night eager to put my new knowledge and insights to work. I planned to get up early and go straight to the studio. But the next morning was unseasonably hot and sunny, so I took a road trip to the seashore. I brought a tube of sunscreen (SPF 50) and was extra careful to cover all exposed parts of my body.

I arrived at the beach and removed my sneakers, even though I was nervous about pieces of sharp litter (my skin provides no protective barrier against glass or metal). I put my feet in the water and was startled by the cold: Gradually it became tolerable, then pleasant.

As I walked, I saw everything through the filter of the previous evening's event. I witnessed a barrage of all sorts of protection, from tattoos, muscles, and cover-ups to bravado and quiet contemplation. By the end of the day, I felt energized and exhausted. I had consumed an emotional, intellectual, and sensory feast.

Armed with a surplus of new perspectives, I returned to my studio with a renewed and expanded desire for introspection. I wondered: Could my art provide protection?

Call and Response

When you finish a body of work, it can be unsettling: You're in a lull, not making work, and you don't know what you want to make next. Perhaps there is a persistent voice in your head asking, "Am I really done? Is there more to explore?"

How do you know when to move on to something new? How do you decide what to leave behind, and what to carry forward?

My last body of work was a sculpture project, created in response to the illness and death of my brother. Some of the discarded pieces resembled fragments of broken statues from an archaeological excavation. They hinted at damaged parts of a puzzle waiting to be restored and reassembled. The art I made at that time was complete, but the materials (and the emotions) were still demanding attention.

My discomfort required action, so I applied for another short residency at the American Academy in Rome, with a proposal to explore the antiquities of ancient Rome and investigate their connections to my own "artifacts." This, I hoped, would help me to move my work to its next stage.

I prepared for my residency by planning a daily itinerary of major sites. But soon after I arrived in Rome, I realized that any progress would require a balance between seeing the sites and disciplined studio time. What I needed was a routine of "Call and Response."

"Call and Response" usually refers to music, where a phrase is called out and an individual or a chorus responds. Now think of it from an artist's point of view: Something calls to you, and you respond by translating that spark of inspiration into physical material.

At the Palazzo Massimo alle Terme, I spent two hours viewing the frescoes that had been found and transported from the ancient walls of the Casa di Livia and the Villa Farnesina. I was attracted to the colors and style of painting, but the call came instead from what was missing: the areas of the frescoes that had been lost. I could see where pieces of history had vanished. Later that day, I went to my studio and made a list of verbs to be used for drawings: cut out, erase, suppress, lose.

More trips yielded more calls for responses. Some excursions were deliberate: I sought out—and was inspired by—historic artifacts that were preserved and protected in museums. But other experiences were unplanned, like coming upon a garden of broken terracotta urns held together by strips that looked like sutures: fasteners to mend what had come apart. Back in the studio, I ripped pieces of paper and then stitched them up using the needle and thread from my mini sewing kit.

One call came not from what I had seen, but from a vivid description by a fellow artist. An architect described his visit to Cuma Antro della Sibilla, near Naples, and showed me photos of an oculus, through which an orb of sunlight poured into the ancient space. In my studio, there was a circular window; every morning, a bright ball of sunlight lit up the wall. My response was not to make anything but simply to pay attention—to glance up every now and then to see how far the orb had crawled.

None of these exercises was meant to lock down a direction, let alone produce finished pieces. Instead, they offered metaphors for the transition from the previous work to the next.

During my last days at the Academy, I borrowed a book on Roman history from the library. I responded to the illustrations by making about thirty quick sketches, and then rubbed the charcoal until there were only traces. I was starting to decide how much to keep, and how much to leave behind.

What Is Broken?

Before I moved out of my last studio, I destroyed a bunch of old work—small plaster sculptures that didn't measure up. I could have just discarded them whole, but instead, I dropped them on the floor and watched how they shattered. Then I gathered the fragments and laid them out on a big table. The jagged shards, with their cracks and rough edges, presented ideas and puzzles, shapes and metaphors.

Most of all, they presented a new perspective. I began to see a broken object not as something to be discarded or rejected, but instead to be considered for how, why, or even if it is broken.

All this rupture was occurring just before a weekend of open studios in my building. I decided to use the opportunity to share my working process with strangers. I wanted feedback and conversation. I would pose this question to each of my visitors: What is broken?

A young woman with a flowered blouse and blue-edged hair came in first and answered without hesitation: "My body." She described her diagnosis of rheumatoid arthritis and her experiences with doctors and medications. She sounded like a detective, determined to be an expert in her own care.

A man and woman came in next. When I asked, "What is broken?" the woman replied, "Our government." We complained together while her partner stood quietly, glancing at the room's tables and walls. Then he said, "My son."

People continued to wander through—individuals, groups of twos or threes or fours, parents and kids. Some conversations lasted a few minutes, some half an hour. We talked about the ways things break—from tangible objects, to hearts, to the world.

I asked a trio of twentysomethings, who were more than eager to weigh in. "We were just talking about this!" one said. She described her workplace, a nonprofit environmental group, where important issues that were supposed to be addressed were overshadowed by technical problems. She was frustrated by the back-and-forth blame game. She sighed. "There are layers of broken."

Then her friend, who is from Ghana and living in Brooklyn, pulled over a chair and sat down. "I work in criminal justice," he said. He talked at length about his family history and his country's problems of sexual abuse and depression in men. "It's not dealt with."

Many visitors answered with a single, objective observation. "Empathy is broken." "Our healthcare system is broken." "Our planet is broken."

Some answers were hopeful: "Broken things regenerate." Some were enigmatic: "Is there broken?"

A woman from Turkey responded to my question with a strong accent. "Broken is energy," she told me. "Chaos is energy. When there is chaos, there is open." As the singer/songwriter Leonard Cohen sang in "Anthem," "There is a crack in everything, that's how the light gets in."

As the afternoon progressed, discussions continued to traverse positive and negative, broken to mended. A woman who had fractured her wrist a year ago described the difficulties of rehabilitation. "But" she added, "while my right hand was healing, I learned to use my left."

I told her I had injured my shoulder, and an MRI had revealed weaknesses that probably existed before and may never fully mend. When she left, I surveyed my table of fragments. An old plaster cast of my arm had split at its weak points. I promised myself I would make a new sculpture with the pieces.

My last open studio visitor was an elderly woman from Germany. When I asked her "What is broken?" she replied, "Today is a different answer from tomorrow."

Walking home from open studios, I stopped to look at the side of a building that displayed a beautiful art installation of twenty-four portraits: giant color photographs with stenciled letters above that read, "All my friends are immigrants and refugees."

A few weeks later, the wall had changed. The portraits were torn away, some partially, some completely. There was no graffiti, just ripped paper outlining the absence of faces, like a negation. It was painful to see that the artist's uplifting message was broken.

Holding Grief

Artists have always dealt with the subject of death and its tributaries of grief. It is perhaps the most ubiquitous topic in art history, with famous representations of mourning ranging from allegorical to religious, autobiographical, and conceptual. Consider Douris's *Eos and Memnon* ancient Greek vase painting, Michelangelo's *Pietà*, Robert Mapplethorpe's *Self Portrait*, and Motoi Yamamoto's installation *Return to the Sea: Saltworks*.

As an artist, you use your practice to translate loss into something new. Your life undergoes a major shift, and you call upon your familiar knowledge: the themes of your past work, your materials and vocabulary, your sensibility and aesthetic. Making art while grieving is a continuation of your artistic practice, with a unique contradiction: the tension between the sweet immersion of creating and the simultaneous pull of sorrow.

To better understand my own process, I wanted to know how other artists use their practice to convert their experience of loss into tangible expression. I had seen the work of the Brooklyn-based artist Nene Humphrey, whose profound performances and installations dealing with mourning moved me long before I had experienced a traumatic loss myself. I asked her to join me for coffee at a favorite neighborhood café.

Nene's expansive, evolving project *Circling the Center* is the very definition of multimedia. She includes drawing, sculpture, video, poetry, music, and performance. This was not always the case.

In 2005, as a long-term artist-in-residence at New York University's LeDoux Lab, Nene had been making drawings based on imagery of the brain's amygdala, an almond-shaped mass with thousands of neurons that help process emotions. A year after she began this work, her husband died unexpectedly of cancer. As she searched for ways to articulate her grief, she happened upon the Victorian art of mourning braiding and was struck by the visual and psychological similarities between the braiding and her drawings. Her artistic practice soon underwent a transformation in depth and breadth.

As we talked, Nene explained the organic ways in which she sought and allowed radical changes to her art making.

"The death of my husband allowed me to get into my work as I never have before," she said. "I still have the core of what I do as an artist. But I never would have taken that many chances. I was so willing to fail—almost not thinking—not rationally plotting it out."

Nene felt the need to make the work richer. "I started to collaborate," she said, "because I didn't know how to do certain things, like video and sound. I was being open to what can happen. [In my previous work,] I had made all the decisions. I had never really collaborated, but now I had willingness. You let go of control." Then she paused and said, "But not *all* control."

I asked Nene about the contradiction of grieving while making art: the feeling of deep sadness juxtaposed with the creative fulfillment of discovering the right expression for the work.

She replied, "You're using the experience; your experience is going into the work."

Then she told me this story:

"When Benny was dying, there was his different breathing, and I went into the room with my tape recorder and recorded it, and then put the recorder away on a shelf. Later, I was talking with my collaborator Roberto [Roberto Carlos Lange, a musician and sound designer] about patterns, and I said, 'I have this tape.' There was a moment when I thought, 'Am I going to tell Roberto about the tape?' But I had to. And he took that sound and used it."

"It's so beautiful," she added, "this rhythmic breathing. I wanted it in there."

A creative practice provides a foundation when we encounter life's painful realities—in particular, losing people we love. We can't predict how difficult times will affect or alter our lives. But as artists, we can call upon, and even expand, our well-honed practice to allow grief to reside in our creative work.

Drawing My Way Through the Pandemic

Every morning, I get up early, just after sunrise, and go downstairs to the kitchen to make coffee. While I wait for the water to boil, I make a drawing on a piece of scrap paper. I add the date and a short caption and then leave it on the counter.

March 21, 2020 Morning sketch: bananas in a bowl. "Last two bananas."

My best friends live in a suburb an hour north of Manhattan. On March 13, we planned a nice weekend—I would come up for a day or two, as I often do to get out of the city. On March 14, COVID-19 accelerated its embrace of New York City, so Paul and Susan, worried about my being on the subway and the Metro-North train, drove to my apartment in Brooklyn to pick me up.

Today is June 23, and I'm still here in Westchester.

All the usual materials and equipment for my work, which is sculpture, are in my studio in Brooklyn. During the first weeks of being away, my creative energy was flat. But the need to make something (anything!) began to nag, and I turned to the loyal foundation of drawing. Even though I stray from a regular practice, every few years something calls me back. Now, the contrasting emotions of gratitude and anxiety, along with the lack of tools other than pencils and my iPad, challenge me to draw again.

March 30, 2020 Morning sketch: kitchen windows, with a view of trees. "So much light in this house!"

Before long, I'm a fixture in our three-person household. Much of our time is spent in separate rooms, immersed in our respective work and Zoom meetings. On rainy afternoons, we gather in the living room and read or listen to the news. Then I get my iPad and draw.

Paul is an easy subject. He doesn't move much. He slouches. His positions are fun to illustrate. Susan, on the other hand, is difficult. She is lying on the couch, wrapped in a knitted blanket, three pillows behind her head, reading on her phone. At first, she is still. But as I attempt to capture a three-quarter view of her profile—especially the bump at the top of her nose—she tilts her head. All the relationships of her face change, and I have to start over. A few minutes later, just as I'm getting the position of her bent knees, she stretches out. I start again.

After fifteen minutes, I stop. I've been focusing so much on her face that I've lost sight of the whole composition, and the drawing is inconsistent: tightly rendered details here; loose, flowing lines there. I hate it. I force myself to do another.

April 4, 2020 Morning sketch: table, cup, and saucer. "I hope to come out of this as a better draftsperson."

I remind myself that drawings need warm-ups. Like an athlete or a musician, I have to ready the instrument. When I settle into a rhythm, I'm looser, and the faster my hand moves, the better. All marks are integral—the best lines sweep across the surface, representing nothing but the pencil sliding from, say, an elbow to a cheekbone. As my dancer friend Martha taught me, it's not the perfect, static position that's important—it's how you get from one position to another.

May 18, 2020 Morning sketch: mask with fruit-pattern fabric. "I can sew more of these."

After a while, I start making detailed drawings of the house's appliances, in particular the ones that I've developed a relationship with. The dishwasher, the washer and dryer, the microwave. When I use them, life feels normal. I draw them straight on and open, as though they are beckoning me to perform routine tasks.

While I draw, my thoughts are nonstop. "The perspective of the top shelf in the refrigerator is off. Is the bottle of milk too big? Did I leave milk in my fridge at home? When will I go home? What is my home?" I erase the bottle and draw it again.

May 31, 2020 Morning sketch: a police car in flames; under that, a glass of wilted purple flowers. "Scary there. Quiet here."

A drawing is doomed if I am too literal, trying to depict a "tree" or a "mouth" or "fingers." The artist Robert Irwin said, "Seeing is forgetting the name of the thing one sees." Sometimes I look for abstract shapes and draw the spaces between them.

June 2, 2020 Morning sketch: a single black rectangle. "#blackouttuesday."

I keep the morning sketches in a drawer. Flipping through them now, along with the drawings on my iPad, I see that what began as a quest to improve my creative skills has become a visual diary of moments ranging from mundane to soul wrenching. Perhaps drawing is my way of confronting—and also escaping—my apprehension about a wildly uncertain future.

June 22, 2020 Morning sketch: mailbox on a wooden post. "Will I get my absentee ballot today?"

Inside Breath

Guided meditation typically begins by paying attention to the breath. It can be straightforward ("Count one as you inhale, two as you exhale") or evocative ("Breathe up from the earth, breathe out to the sky"). Either way, the goal is to focus on a single action, an automatic bodily function that we usually ignore.

At least that's how it used to be. But in March 2020, this country began its battle with COVID-19. In the three years that followed, I thought more about breath than in all my years combined. The seemingly simple subject of breath became exhausting.

We collectively watched the extremes of life-giving and life-taking. We saw essential workers putting themselves at risk to keep others breathing. Even in mundane activities, breath was a constant and troubling consideration. When you checked the weather to see if you could enjoy a socially distanced visit with a friend, the real question you were asking was, "Can we avoid sharing breath?"

A stranger's close-range exhalation could trigger complex emotions. One week, in Trader Joe's, I came upon a woman who was maskless. She was breathing heavily. My immediate reaction was to turn my back on her, which made me feel horrible. A moment later, I was angry. How dare she endanger everyone around her? Then I worried that she might have asthma or a heart condition. My conflicted thoughts came from ten seconds of standing in three square feet of shared oxygen.

On my daily walks through urban streets, I became keenly aware of windows and their visceral effect on my body. I surveyed the modern skyscrapers, with their unopenable, full-floor sheets of glass, and I felt my chest tighten. I got anxious when I was sealed in a room with other people and there was no access to outside air.

In contrast, I gained a new perspective on buildings that I know and love. Simmons Hall, an MIT dormitory designed by Steven Holl Architects, has always delighted my eyes; now it was delighting my respiratory system. Strolling by one afternoon, I saw a young woman coming out the front door, and I asked her if she liked the building. "Oh, yes!" she said. "Especially the windows." Each of the dorm's single rooms has at least nine operable windows, and they open out at all angles. Looking up at them from the street, they are like flocks of giddy, wide-winged birds.

As a city dweller, those years made me appreciate the outdoors more than ever; I breathe deeply when I enter green gardens and leafy parks. It's not surprising that many early urban parks were created for the public in response to disease. For example, the design of New York's Central Park, by Frederick Law Olmsted and Calvert Vaux, began in 1858, in the aftermath of New York's second cholera outbreak. Olmsted believed that public parks should function as the "lungs of the city," and that "the occasional contemplation of natural scenes . . . in connection with change of air and change of habits, is favourable to the health and vigour of men." When I read that Olmsted's first child died of cholera at two months, and his brother John died of tuberculosis at thirty-two, I was reminded that great gifts to the population are often borne from personal loss.

The COVID-19 years came with more all-encompassing, simultaneous unknowns than I have ever encountered—for myself, for my family and friends, and for the country. Now, when it seems that nothing is secure, I tell myself how lucky I am: I can still control my breath.

I invite you to join me: Close your eyes, breathe up from the earth, and breathe out to the sky.

4 PEOPLE

Like teenagers, my new drawings seek approval and then question it. They're afraid of being exposed, but they want to be seen. They want to be let out of my studio and hear voices other than the ones inside my head.

The Talented Audience

When I attend a performance, I like to arrive early so I can watch the show before the show—that is, the audience. At a dance concert at the Joyce Theater in New York City, I spotted, just a few rows in front of me, Mikhail Baryshnikov. After the initial shock of being starstruck, I looked around and realized that the audience was filled with an abundance of talent: dancers coming to see dancers, not only to hone their craft and to observe the hottest new choreography, but also to share, as a group, the sheer love of dance.

As I continued to take in the crowd, I imagined all the other kinds of artists that must be there—musicians, writers, visual artists, actors. I felt a surge of pride: I am a member of this talented audience! But the talent I'm referring to is not that of single individuals who, one by one, have a particular gift or genius. Instead, I am talking about a talented *body* of many interdependent parts, like a complex organism that inherently knows that each cell contributes to the mutual support that makes it a gifted entity. We were all there with the common hope and expectation of being nourished and stimulated. It is not just what I see on the stage that makes me feel so . . . well . . . that makes me feel, period. It is being in a community of strangers that shares this passion.

The New York Public Library has a series called "Live from the NYPL," which has been described as "provocative conversations, real debates, irresistible performances, original ideas." One of the events I attended was "Lena Herzog in Conversation with Lawrence Weschler." The subject was Herzog's monograph *Lost Souls*, a photographic investigation of the cabinets of wonder and curiosities (*Kunstkammern and Wunderkammern*) that include the world's earliest medical museums.

The dialogue was about an artist's journey of creating tender and unsettling photographs. But it was also about philosophy, history, poetry, religion, science, immortality, and fear. The conversation itself was a performance: The repartee between Weschler, a brilliant and prolific author of creative nonfiction, and Herzog, a broadly educated and inspired artist, was scintillating, both zinging historical references or reciting animated excerpts from Nabokov, Szymborska, and Sartre. There was no way to know if the audience was keeping up, but I noticed that many were doing the same thing I was: frantically scribbling notes to Google later.

After the event, which lasted two hours, plus another half hour for book purchasing and signing, we were all invited to attend a reception at the International Center of Photography (back then, a two-minute walk from the library), where Herzog's photographs were being exhibited. As we traveled en masse from Fifth Avenue to Sixth, I was pleased to be in the company of others, carrying the same heavy books and going in together for another round.

This all got me thinking about other talented audiences. At the Museum of Modern Art (MoMA) exhibit *The Artist Is Present* in 2010, the performance artist Marina Abramović sat all day, silent and barely moving, throughout the duration of the show (more than seven hundred hours total). On a first-come, first-served basis, museum visitors sat, also silently, in a chair facing her. According to *The New York Times*, "the chair has rarely, if ever, been empty. Close to 1,400 people have occupied it, some for only a minute or two, a few for an entire day."

During the show, the photographer Marco Anelli took portraits of every visitor who participated in the piece. The portraits were on MoMA's website (and are now in a book by Anelli), and scrolling through them, one could see the visceral reaction of each person experiencing intense, private moments in a very public place. I checked into the site often, and as the weeks passed, it was clear that although Abramović's endurance was riveting, it was the members of the audience who made that exhibit so compelling. Each person had chosen and shared the same act: confronting Abramović's unwavering stare, all without movement, sound, or comment.

The word "audience" implies a passive, inactive body. Its antonym is "participant." But a talented audience is always participating. Even when it is silent and still.

What
Artists
Know

I was having a tough time in my studio. After January 20, 2017 (Trump's first inauguration), my inner critic became more vocal than usual: "Your art is too personal, self-indulgent, and, worse yet, irrelevant!" I was obsessed with questions: Do I leave my current work behind, and instead make art that is explicitly political? Or do I close the door (and my ears) and remain true to the art I have been making for decades? What artist am I now?

I put these questions on hold when I joined friends to march and sign petitions and make phone calls in protest. During one of our sessions of group letter-writing, we commiserated that many of our actions would be met with defeat rather than victory. But we vowed to keep at it.

Later, when I got back to my studio to work on a series I had been struggling with, it occurred to me that staying committed in the face of repeated failure is nothing new to artists. Our standards are high, because we set them ourselves. (Tell me, who is more demanding than you are of yourself?) Our efforts often fall short, but we keep working to achieve the small percentage that exceeds our expectations.

Ironically, that ability to tolerate failure makes artists the perfect population to endure the repeated long slogs of upholding our country's values. It's just one of the seemingly contradictory attributes that make artists uniquely qualified to keep fighting.

Along with being adept at failure, we are patient. We know that it can take months or years to get a response to our work. We handle rejection, insults, and judgments. We persevere.

My first impulse after the 2017 inauguration was to alter my art and make it more political. I tried to commandeer work that I had started with a different intention and ended up flattening it into a superficial—and false—gesture. I threw it in the dumpster. But after a few weeks, I realized that my work would unavoidably undergo change. My project had begun two years earlier, in response to a single person's circumstance. It was about the body's frailties and the desire to protect and to be protected. I began to see the series in the context of a wider population than just my family. The personal is indeed political.

Artists are not only creators; we are also ambassadors of art, and we can convey its power to others. In her January 18, 2017 article in *The Nation* titled "What Art Under Trump?" author Margaret Atwood wrote: "Fifty years from now, what will be said about the art and writing of this era? The Great Depression was immortalized by John Steinbeck's *Grapes of Wrath*. . . . Arthur Miller's play *The Crucible* provided an apt metaphor for McCarthyism. . . . What sorts of novels, poems, films, television series, video games, paintings, music, or graphic novels will adequately reflect America's next decade?"

Often, the most profound impact our art can deliver comes from our audience. Art that allows viewers or readers or listeners to bring their own authorship goes deeper and lasts longer. It also provides a more effective call to action than didactic sermonizing.

On January 20, 2017, a group of activists known as Occupy Museums presented "Artists Speak Out" at the Whitney Museum in Manhattan. Approximately thirty-two artists/art groups/institutions gave short presentations. The speakers were eloquent and passionate. But for me, the most powerful presentation was not a speech; it was an artwork: a musical composition by Tracie Morris and Vijay Iyer. Morris briefly introduced the piece as being " . . . from a lovely musical . . . it's about feeling better when you're afraid, when fascists are at the door."

Iyer's piano rumbled behind Morris's mesmerizing repetition of single words and short phrases: "Raindrops. Raindrops and whiskers. Girls in white, boys in white. Tied up with string. . . . When the dogs bite. I simply remember, I simply remember."

Behind the piano, a huge window framed the Hudson River. This is a view that I treasure. It is one of *my* favorite things. As I listened, I recalled a quote by the artist Ai Weiwei, speaking of contemporary Beijing: "There are no places that you relate to, that you love to go. . . . Everything is constantly changing, according to somebody else's will, somebody else's power."

An artist's creative practice is rooted in all these attributes, from the personal to the political. They are our contribution to society, and they are needed now. We read and hear, many times over, the pronouncement: "Art is more important than ever." Please consider an even larger truth: *Artists* are more important than ever.

Twin Art Histories

Why does the eye love what it loves? How is visual taste formed? How deeply entrenched is it?

For most artists, it's a mystery why we gravitate to one style of art over another—why we use vibrant colors or work only in black and white; why we favor abstraction versus realism; why we strive for simplicity or relish the baroque. There are millions of influences, from our earliest exposure to art as children, to our education through institutions, to osmosis through contemporary culture. There are styles and aesthetics that we absorb, and, consciously or not, tend to mimic. They feel "right."

But taking a closer look at my visual tendencies, I'm surprised by what I've discovered about how they were formed, particularly when it comes to art history.

When I started working in sculpture, I visited the vast galleries of ancient Greek and Roman antiquity at the Metropolitan Museum of Art in New York. The main, barrel-vaulted gallery is filled with gleaming white marble figures, all bathed in natural light. Here were the statues I'd studied in Art History 101—rock stars of antiquity, all within inches of me. I visited the galleries repeatedly; the sculptures' power and allure, already embedded in my consciousness, gained an even stronger foothold.

Then I came across an article titled "The Myth of Whiteness in Classical Sculpture" by Margaret Talbot. She describes the well-known but persistently ignored truth about Greek and Roman marble figures: Most were originally painted in their entirety, and the colors were bright. In fact, based on historical documentation, along with technologies capable of identifying remaining pigments, the presence of color is now indisputable.

Polychromy—the painting of objects in various hues—in ancient sculpture was first discovered by those who performed the earliest excavations in the cities surrounding Mount Vesuvius. But most of what has been excavated over the years has appeared to be devoid of color. Because of its exposure to the elements, the paint chipped off, and in many cases, the remaining traces of color were washed away, as restorers and excavators eagerly cleaned what had been unearthed. As Talbot writes, "In the nineteen-thirties, restorers at the British Museum polished the Elgin marbles"—a collection of sculptures from Athens—". . . until they were as white and shiny as pearls."

The researcher Vinzenz Brinkmann, who has been studying polychromy since the 1980s, has used technology to determine original colors. Talbot writes that in the 1990s, he and his wife, Ulrike Koch-Brinkmann, began recreating sculptures in plaster, resulting in a touring exhibition titled *Gods in Color*. Talbot describes a statue on view: "A Trojan archer, from approximately 500 B.C., wears tight pants with a harlequin pattern that is as boldly colored as Missoni leggings."

I began to recollect studies revealing antiquity's colorful past that I had heard about but forgotten. I had absorbed the myth that the sculpture of Greek and Roman antiquity was pure white. I was curious to learn more, so I found the book *Gods in Color: Polychromy in the Ancient World*, which was co-edited by Brinkmann and his wife, along with Renée Dreyfus.

The beautifully produced hardcover is filled with reproductions of what sculptures might have looked like. The "old," i.e., classical, white versions are shown alongside the color reproductions. It was jarring. The colors felt garish, the faces cartoon-like. I suddenly pictured the bright gallery at the Metropolitan Museum of Art, no longer full of gleaming white figures but instead transformed, full of these vividly painted sculptures. It seemed impossible to erase my gut reaction of disapproval.

What happens when we revisit history and identify a mistake in how our aesthetic vision was formed? Do we stop and recalibrate? Are we able to undo what has been ingrained? Is it possible to retrain our eye and intercept prejudgments?

On the radio program *On the Media*, Brooke Gladstone interviewed the writer John Keene about his collection of stories and novellas, *Counternarratives*. Keene remarks, "I was very interested in histories that are totally hidden, totally buried, totally obscured." He tells Gladstone, "History never happens in isolation. Every story has a twin."

Though Keene was talking about race and slavery, his words can be applied to any historical narrative. The question of how we acquire visual taste is not a superficial one. The aesthetics that we learn matter. When we are trained to see what is "right"—what is beautiful and tasteful and classical—anything else can seem less worthy, or worse, repugnant.

When one history dominates, it obscures and even erases the others. If I had been exposed to different histories, would I be a different artist?

Looking
at
Artists
Looking

Yoko Ono is famous because she was married to John Lennon. But long before she met him, she was creating groundbreaking performance art. Her exhibition at MoMA titled *Yoko Ono: One Woman Show, 1960–1971* included a film of *Cut Piece*, performed in 1965 at Carnegie Recital Hall.

In the film, Ono sits before an audience in her black dress, a giant pair of scissors on the floor in front of her. She has instructed audience members to cut pieces of her clothing to take away. As they comply with her wishes—some with hesitation, others with glee—Ono remains steely-faced, staring straight ahead.

There have been many interpretations of this work, from a feminist statement to a seductive striptease. For me, it was about courage, a quality that I regard as important and difficult to achieve in any creative endcavor.

Hungry to learn more, I researched the background of *Cut Piece* and found an essay Ono had written, originally published in 1974 in the Japanese magazine *Bungei Shunjū*. "Instead of giving the audience what the artist chooses to give," she wrote, "the artist gives what the audience chooses to take. . . . [Y]ou cut and take whatever part you want . . . when I sat on stage in front of the audience, I felt that this was my genuine contribution."

Ono was talking about generosity. This was her objective, but it was definitely not my takeaway. For me, *Cut Piece* was a challenge to be brave. I learned from Ono that whatever she gave, I would somehow choose what to take. Ono's performance made me think about my own art. Do I show courage, or have I become complacent?

You can study an artist's intention, a critic's judgment, and a historian's scholarliness, but all pale in comparison to the message that a work of art can give you for your own art making. Your favorite artists—whether contemporary or ancient—can provide more than inspiration; you can use their art to examine your own work.

The Metropolitan Museum of Art (the Met) has an online series of short videos called *The Artist Project*, in which artists were invited to choose and respond to works in the museum's collection. Each video shows an artist standing with the art they have chosen to discuss. The artists are familiar with the details and context of the work and have absorbed what they need to support their own artistic directions. Often, the "message" they have gleaned is a far cry from the work's original purpose.

Rona Pondick selected Egyptian sculpture fragments. Pondick knows these fragments well; she grew up in New York, spent a lot of time in the Met's Egyptian galleries, and has used body fragments in her own work for more than thirty years.

As Pondick looks at a broken off piece of a face or torso or hand, she tries to imagine how she would make it—not as a reproduction of its original state, but instead as the current fragment, as though that was the way it was meant to be. "The fragment is so resonant and powerful," she says. "What's not there informs what is there."

Pondick has identified what she needs for her work. "I know I look very differently than an art historian does. I'm a maker, so the first thing I ask myself is how is this made? If I had to make this now, how would I make it?"

I have just written approximately six hundred words encouraging you to take away your own unique meaning, regardless of the creator's original intent. But sometimes the artist's vision is exactly the one you need to hear.

When I first saw Monique Johannet's diptych painting *For-give me. Again?*, I thought it was about relationships; I admired it but did not relate it to my own work. At a later time, I had the opportunity to ask Johannet about the painting, and she told me that it is about a relationship, but not the kind I had imagined. Instead, it represented a conversation with her studio in which she is apologizing for being away and neglecting her practice . . . again.

I, too, had been away from my studio for too long. I wanted, and needed, to change that. Johannet's intention hit me loud and clear, as inspiration, challenge, and even encouragement. That painting now hangs in my home, and my response to it changes often, depending on my relationship to my work.

The more deeply you look at a favorite artwork, the more likely you are to find its significance for your creative practice. Keep looking, and a message from the artist will, in some way, come through.

As Ono said, " . . . the artist gives what the audience chooses to take."

Outside Conversations

New York's Metropolitan Museum of Art houses reconstructed frescoes from the ancient Roman villa at Boscoreale, an area about a mile north of Pompeii. During a visit to the Met, I saw the frescoes and was struck by their familiarity, even though I had never seen them before. Then it hit me: Their edges reminded me of a Mark Rothko painting. I Googled Rothko and Boscoreale on my phone and read that on his frequent visits to the Met, Rothko had been deeply moved by these wall paintings.

It had been a while since I had seen the Rothko paintings, so I decided to visit them, not only to reconnect, but also to connect anew. I went to the galleries of modern and contemporary art and found his *No. 21*, an abstract painting of deep red with slate blue underpainting. Standing before it, my feelings for Rothko's work were intensified. Because I had made a connection between Rothko and the villa's frescoes, I felt that I had entered an ongoing dialogue between an artist and another work of art. It was an unexpected conversation between artists dead and alive, and I was a witness.

Most summers, I visit a friend in Maine. Her shelves hold an eclectic assortment of books left by previous guests, and on a rainy day, I surveyed the spines and pulled out a fat, musty book with a faded cover: *Remembrance of Things Past, Volume I* by Marcel Proust.

I read the first few sentences. "For a long time, I used to go to bed early. Sometimes, when I had put out my candle, my eyes would close so quickly that I had not even time to say to myself: 'I'm falling asleep.'" Over the next six pages, the narrator describes in detail the experience of the night, including musings about dreams, memories, and feelings: " . . . when I awoke in the middle of the night, not knowing where I was, I could not even be sure at first who I was." The sentences were dense, long, and difficult to read, and after about twenty pages, I put the book back on the shelf.

That night, I went to bed very early. I fell asleep within seconds of turning out the light. I woke up in the middle of the night, confused about where I was. Suddenly I recollected, in surprising detail, the few pages I had read of *Remembrance of Things Past*. Before falling back to sleep, I promised myself I would give it another try.

My next morning in Maine, I went into town and passed by the library. The previous night was still fresh in my mind, and on a whim, I decided to look for a biography of Proust. I found a slim one by Edmund White, skimmed through it, and came upon a reference to Proust's "The Confession of a Young Girl." In the story, the fourteen-year-old character repeatedly calls her mother back to her bedside to say goodnight, inventing ever-new pretexts such as the necessity to turn her hot pillow over. I stopped short. Years ago, I read a story by David Foster Wallace in which he described how his mother used to change the pillowcases whenever he was sick in bed so that they were clean and cool. He referred to "the feeling of turning a pillow over to the cool side." Published posthumously after Wallace's suicide, that story comes to mind almost every hot summer night when I turn my own pillow over to its cool side. As I left the library, I wondered if Wallace had read that story by Proust, and was struck again by how an unexpected conversation among White, Proust, Wallace, and myself had deepened my connection to works of art—in this case, to the writing of both Proust and Wallace.

What elicits a bond with a work of art? My experience with Rothko and the Roman frescoes was the opposite of what happened when I picked up *Remembrance of Things Past*. I already knew and loved Rothko's work and was eager to go further. Proust, on the other hand, was intimidating; I had no connection, and my curiosity was not based on a desire but rather a "should." However, in both cases, an unexpected "conversation" occurred—not with the work itself, but away from it. It was the connection between artists that made me return to the paintings and books to know them more deeply.

There are abundant resources that can intensify one's experience of a work of art, encouraging another, even deeper visit. I'm the first to sign up for a lecture or a docent tour, or to listen to an audio guide that increases my knowledge about a particular artwork. But for me, it is the unseen conversations that occur outside of the work that bring me back to it.

Scouting Ideas from Other Artists

I headed to the exhibition *Modigliani Unmasked* at the Jewish Museum in Manhattan with a single goal: to improve my own figure drawings. I wanted to push them beyond their minimalist style, but I didn't want to lose their simplicity. I found my inspiration in a black crayon sketch: *Female Nude with a Lighted Candle and Chandeliers*, inspired by Anna Akhmatova. Amedeo Modigliani caught the figure's gesture concisely and elegantly with an outline. Then he added a contradiction: short, messy lines encasing the outline like a coarse cloak. In my drawing session later that day, I remembered Modigliani's rough marks: They did not negate simplicity; they embraced it.

Each time I visit an art exhibition, it is more than an enjoyable pastime—it's a necessary pursuit. My focus depends on the challenges I'm confronting in my own art making. It can be stylistic, like studying Modigliani's use of line. It can be pragmatic, like hunting for lighting solutions and display possibilities. Or it can be theoretical, like exploring language that will help me articulate the impetus for my new body of work.

During a project consisting of small sculptures, my studio was the scene of a population explosion: The pieces were jumbled together, overcrowded on shelves and tables. They would soon be moving from this private room to public spaces, and they needed to be presented as a physically compelling entity. But how?

I visited the Marian Goodman Gallery to see Cristina Iglesias's installation *Phreatic Zones*, a sculpture that is more like architecture—a terraced structure that occupies most of a large room. It's an inside river: Water flows over aluminum forms that look like glowing, tangled tree roots.

Iglesias's installation provoked a surge of thoughts about presentation. First, it sparked practical ideas beyond any I had previously considered: Should I incorporate metallic materials? Add hidden lights? Vary the level of the floor? Second, I was inspired by the atmosphere Iglesias had created; the space energized me and transported me out of the present. In an article in the *Huffington Post*, Iglesias said, "I use [water] as a material that marks time, that changes, that makes a sound even within its silence, and that makes the places build active."

When I went to the MoMA to see the exhibition *Louise Bourgeois: An Unfolding Portrait*, I expected to continue in the same vein—that is, focusing on physical aspects. I've always been attracted to Bourgeois's courageous sculptures and installations—they are big, bold, and beautifully constructed.

But her prints and books raised a different set of questions about presentation. If your art comes from a private and emotional place, how much of that story do you want to explicitly reveal?

Bourgeois never shied away from relating her personal narratives; in fact, she insisted that you know them. Some are literally printed on the pages of her fabric illustrated books—works that reference the tapestries that were the focus of her family's business when she was a child. The pages of *Ode à la Bièvre* and *Hours of the Day* contain text from her diaries: "I had gone back with my children to . . . see the house where I had grown up and where the river Bièvre flowed. . . ." and "I am on the other side of despair and this happens to me four times a day." For me, her words are compelling because they are simultaneously specific and universal.

I recently showed an acquaintance images of my sculptures—broken casts of my hands embedded in slabs and blocks—and her response was: "Eeeww. Stunning, but creepy."

Then I told her about my impetus: It was a combination of my brother's terminal illness and my own mild autoimmune disorder. "Ah," she said. "That changes everything."

At first, I was hurt. Isn't the art supposed to speak for itself? We want the power to come from the work, not from the story about the work. But unexplained art, while strong on its own, may not convey the artist's intended message. So ask yourself: How much of your backstory do you want to tell? Will your explanation help viewers understand what they are seeing? Or will it provide too much direction, steering them away from finding their own meaning?

Days after a museum expedition, I can recall the artworks that I focused on while I was there. But the specific lessons that I gained from each artist—about style or presentation or narrative— change, often leaking into the other categories. I picture Modigliani's drawing, and I think about his identity as an Italian Sephardic Jew in Paris. Conversely, I recollect Bourgeois's emotional text on a handkerchief, and I wonder how I might use fabric in an installation.

Beyond the Syllabus

I remember the first day of the first studio class I taught. I handed out my syllabus and walked the students through the assignments, exercises, and readings. I emphasized the collaborative nature of the class, explaining that their most creative work would come from mutual support.

Then I launched into a typical first activity: I asked them to introduce themselves one by one and describe their most recent projects. As we progressed, the students who had not yet spoken seemed distracted, their attention directed inward. I realized they were probably concentrating on what they would say about themselves. I had spent weeks perfecting the syllabus, and then, almost immediately, thwarted one of my primary goals, which was to encourage the students to listen to and learn from each other.

Those of you who are teachers know that your detailed syllabus is only the beginning of determining how you will teach your subject. Beyond the syllabus, and even beyond your day-to-day lesson plan, you need to design the classroom experience.

Think about the underlying factors that will affect your goals. How do physical space and movement influence class participation? Do you consider pacing, so that students are at times animated, and at other times contemplative? What about maintaining energy during a class that lasts for three, or even four hours? These subtleties affect the overall experience, and it's best not to leave them to chance.

After that first year of teaching, I redesigned the introduction process. Now I begin by pairing up students and asking them to interview each other, and then report back to the class. I remind them that they are responsible for representing each other accurately and compellingly. I also tell them to pay attention to how they are being described, because they will most likely get a new perspective on their work.

I've done this now for years, and every time, I'm impressed not only with the consideration that the students give each other, but also with the way they become invested in each other's work.

We're all conscious of the dip in concentration that tends to occur midway through a long crit (critique) session. But in a recent photography class, I noticed that the lethargy could be attributed to factors other than length of time. For the first two weeks, we projected the students' images. As the crit progressed, it occurred to me that even though the screen was active, we were all sitting motionless in a dark room, moving only our mouths and eyes, and one lone finger on the keyboard.

So for the third week, I asked the students to bring physical prints. We spread them out, and we moved around the table, reaching across to re-sequence the prints, suggesting edits and groupings. It felt much more alive; we were all physically and spatially involved with the work.

I'm not suggesting that you revert to an analog classroom. I'm saying that ignoring physicality and space is also ignoring energy.

Back in the mid-1990s, I taught a class on user interface design. I was always on the lookout for ways to encourage brainstorming, so when I happened to meet an improvisational theater actor, I invited him to lead us in a workshop. The students paired up—one representing a technology with a specific personality, the other representing a user—and performed a series of hilarious and enlightening encounters with a sleazy elevator, an arrogant ATM, an empathetic alarm clock, and a stupid VCR.

I was delighted with the session, because it brought concepts like empathy and arrogance into the vocabulary of interface design. But as I look back at how the students learned, I see that a big part of the workshop's success was that we were playful. Ideas came and went spontaneously, with no time wasted on preciousness.

My ongoing challenge is to be clear about my intentions: I want to deliver a direction but also encourage the students to follow their own. One standout moment was when a student complained that I encouraged them to do anything, and yet I seemed to be expecting something specific. This was an eye-opener, reminding me that teaching is a balancing act that requires communication.

A classroom is like theater, where all participants are performers. The array of factors—time, space, energy, support, pacing, and more—are necessary considerations that go far beyond the syllabus.

Yes,
and...
Yes,
But

I am a greedy teacher. If you're an educator, you can probably relate. Sure, you want to inspire your students, imparting your own knowledge and pushing them beyond set boundaries. But don't you also hope that they will inspire changes in you?

Judith Tannenbaum, the Curator of Contemporary Art at the RISD Museum, asked me to create an exhibition about public privacy: how urban citizens create private mental zones when they are alone in public. I was excited about having the show at RISD, a community of creative artists in diverse disciplines, and I wanted to use the opportunity to challenge myself to think differently about a topic I had been involved with for more than eight years. After a brainstorming discussion with Judith, we agreed: What better way than to teach a Wintersession class as a way to develop the exhibition?

My goal for the course was twofold: first, to teach a subject and a methodology for investigating it, and second, to see if, through the students, I could see my material in new ways.

The syllabus for the class was based on "Yes, and . . . ", a technique borrowed from improvisational theater. Its premise is that you accept and then build on each other's ideas. For six weeks, we collaborated in changing groups of two or three or four. Through a series of exercises—from observing, to sketching, to brainstorming and model-making—each day's work provided the fodder to advance to the next.

The first week introduced the concept of the inward gaze. We went to the RISD library, a beautiful building with innovative spaces designed to encourage solitary creative thinking. I asked the students to sit for half an hour, documenting what provided support for contemplation, and what did not.

A primary aspect of public privacy is how we use personal technology to create a cocoon when we're in public spaces: We employ laptops and earbuds and smartphones to retreat from our surroundings. But when my students returned from the library, they pointed out that personal technology—a cell phone ring, an email or text alert—was what took them out of their contemplative space. For me, this was a new perspective: While our devices can help us construct a mental seclusion, they can also break into it.

To explore this idea further, I asked my students to make one-minute videos of themselves working alone in a public place, such as a café. When I watched the results, I was surprised to find subtle but distinct gestures common to all of them: a furrowed brow; a coffee cup lifted and held for a moment, as though supporting an unfinished thought; occasional eye contact with fellow café-mates. Building on these studies, we listed eight gestures from the videos and recreated them as a choreographed video recital.

This series of activities made me realize that I had considered the mind's eye as an invisible, unshared mental state that separated city dwellers. Now I saw that if I watched people more closely, I would find a commonality and mutual awareness in physical movements.

Throughout the class, I relied on "Yes, and . . . " to generate new points of view. By presenting an idea, and then observing and incorporating the students' responses, I was able to expand how I think about public privacy.

During the six weeks, based on my previous experience of building a blog to document the process of creating new work, I decided to use that technique to document class activities and assignments. We took a slew of photographs of the class in action, from serious concentration to bursts of laughter, and of the work in progress: sketches and models, some realistic, others extreme and absurd. All were important. The blog was a vessel, a place where we could reflect on what we had done. Our entire process was visible.

At the end of Wintersession, as we looked at the blog together, some of the students expressed concern about showing what they considered their "bad" work—that is, half-baked ideas or quickly drawn sketches. One student suggested that I curate the blog, selecting only the best work.

I immediately and vehemently vetoed the suggestion. I said, "It already *is* curated. It's curated to track how we evolved and where ideas came from." To omit any piece would negate our process of each idea building on the previous one. I wanted to express my convictions about what I should not change. I found myself saying "Yes, but . . ." rather than "Yes, and . . ."

My student's response was equally forceful. "You already have a presence on the internet, and you have presented yourself the way you want to. We are students, and our presence is still unformed. We need to have some control."

They were right. I had missed this. Together, we decided that we would keep the blog as it was, but we would restrict its access to our class only.

I wanted my students to inspire me and change my perspective about public privacy, and they did. What I did not expect was that they would also help me to remove my blinders.

Advancing Collaboration

I love letterpress. So, while working on a printmaking project that included brief lines of text, I decided that the type should be set by hand—*my* hand. I was at a month-long residency at Women's Studio Workshop, which provided the equipment and supplies I needed. But after a week of frustrated attempts, all I produced was a big mess. What I really needed was an expert.

When I returned home, I found and commissioned a letterpress printer—a sole practitioner who had a studio behind his house. I was careful to provide clear specifications, and he carried them out perfectly. His deep familiarity with type, paper, ink, and presses came from years of work. I was more than satisfied with the finished pages, grateful for their technical precision.

A few months later, I went back to the printer's studio to pick up leftover paper. I'd been there only once, because I'd extracted myself from the hands-on aspects of printing. On this visit, I realized that I had overlooked the lively array of diverse equipment, materials, proofs, and vestiges of his other projects—exuberant collaborations with poets and visual artists.

As I left the studio with packages of blank sheets, I wondered: By focusing so starkly on a specific outcome, had I missed an opportunity? Was there another part of the project waiting to be explored? My narrow definition of "commission" had excluded "collaboration." When you seek another artist's expertise, you should, of course, respect their turf. But that doesn't mean you have to remove yourself from it.

My next venture involved a very different medium: live performance. My role was to develop visual components of moving imagery and typography for a theatrical production. I wanted to use computer-based tools to experiment, and I needed technical expertise to code and build the software and hardware.

I had the good luck to meet Michael Chladil, then a graduate student at New York University's Interactive Telecommunications Program. Michael was working on his thesis, a "modular system for media playback that consisted of ropes and pulleys that people could use to control recorded loops of music." In other words, use your body to move the music.

Michael decided to do an internship with me, during which he would expand his programming to incorporate video and text segments. I was determined to go beyond my previously myopic view of expertise, so a large chunk of our meetings consisted of us talking about our interests. The more I learned about Michael's background and creative pursuits, the more I saw how our goals overlapped. We both wanted to make work that brought spirited physical action to technology.

During the next two years, Michael and I developed tools and practices that went far beyond our initial plans. When I was asked to create an exhibition at the gallery@calit2, now known as Gallery QI, at the University of California San Diego, I invited Michael to join me as co-artist. The result was *Overheard*, an interactive installation that I could not have imagined without our years of collaboration.

Now, when I see the work of artists who have commissioned outside expertise, I look for the evidence of erased boundaries. I try to imagine how both artists have gone beyond the early technical specifications and have allowed their shared openness to nurture their imaginations. In the best cases, the mutual influence goes so far as to blend—and even reverse—the predefined roles.

I found a famous example at the *Picasso Sculpture* show at

MoMA: the wire constructions that Pablo Picasso made with the sculptor Julio González. It's hard to say where Picasso's "commission" stage— i.e., the early ideas he brought to be built—morphed into collaborative experimentation, but who cares? The results are what matter.

In a gallery that included metal sculptures made in González's studio, the wall text explained the artists' fluid roles: "González welcomed Picasso into his small metalworking studio in Montparnasse, where he straddled the roles of tutor and assistant, at first translating into wire Picasso's line drawings of 1928, and eventually partnering with him on the complicated planes and angles of the constructions of 1929–1931."

A 1956 MoMA press release for González's first exhibition in the United States describes Picasso's influence on the sculptor: "'From this collaboration,' Mr. Ritchie (Director of the Museum's Department of Painting and Sculpture) says, 'one can only conclude that the greatest inventor of imagery in the twentieth century transmitted a new vision to his old friend and technical advisor.'"

It's smart to come to an expert with a specific goal and clear specifications for your vision. But if you approach a project with too much clarity, you run the risk of missing an opportunity. Instead, consider letting the expertise of both sides blur. You might move on to achieve something unexpected that changes both of you.

Exposing New Work

I've been making new drawings on my iPad. They're simple and colorful, and they don't resemble anything I've done before. I enjoy making them, but each one underwhelms me. They feel immature. I complained to a friend: "My drawings are very young." She grinned and said, "What, like seven?"

Actually, they are more like teenagers—insecure and self-conscious. And like teenagers, they seek approval and then question it. They're afraid of being exposed, but they want to be seen. Even though the work is tentative, there's a point when it wants to be let out and hear voices other than the ones inside my head.

As an artist, when your work enters an unfamiliar realm where you don't have experience or a track record, you might be hesitant about showing it to anyone.

I brought up these issues of exposure and vulnerability with a colleague who is an accomplished author. She told me about her writing group, which has been meeting every other week for fifteen years to read aloud and critique what they are working on. I asked how the feedback affects her.

"Once I put something new out to the group, I turn my judgment over to them," she said. "Sometimes, if one member is unimpressed, I have trouble hearing anything positive from the others. I have to find my way back to believing them." Then she added, "Whether it's positive or negative, all of their feedback is legitimate. They know what they are talking about."

A few years ago, I was at an artist residency where, each evening, one artist presented to the other residents. On the day of my presentation, I told a colleague that I was going to show—i.e., expose—the videos I had just made. She said, "You're showing new work? How brave!" Her warning was prescient. I had hoped to gain perspective, but later, when I presented, one audience member's harsh comment overshadowed all others. Because my work was untested and vulnerable, his remark derailed me. It took me a couple of days before I was able to let his casual criticism go and return to my experiments.

How we accept (or dismiss) responses about new work is important. But to fully understand the feedback we're getting, we need to acknowledge the environment in which it is delivered and received.

During the pandemic, the only way that most artists saw one another's work in progress was on a screen. I attended several artist presentations on Zoom, where some participants had their video turned off. Was their attention divided? Were they making dinner? Folding laundry?

And then there's Instagram. I've had many valuable interactions with other artists on the platform, and it's been useful as a destination, a place for my young drawings to put a toe in the water. But that water is murky.

We all know that the number of "likes" is an unreliable measurement of how an audience feels, not only because social media algorithms prioritize certain content over others, but also because viewing is, by nature, so casual. The other day I watched someone rhythmically glide through Instagram: scroll, double tap, scroll, double tap. Did she look at anything?

Showing new work, on the other hand, is anything but casual for an artist. When we put something out there, we seek a response, and it's nearly impossible not to be affected by the numbers. Why does this drawing get more likes than that one? Are my other drawings unlikeable? Should I delete them? As a software engineer once advised me, "Beware of making art to appease the algorithm."

But what if I am shaping the work for a particular platform without even realizing it? This occurred to me when, in the middle of making a new drawing, I stopped because I thought, "Oh, that won't look good on Instagram."

After sixteen months of the pandemic's enforced seclusion, I had an IRL studio visit with a long-time friend. We both wanted to show each other our new work, and we took our time, luxuriating in four hours of looking and talking. When she left, I felt elated, not because of positive reactions—we barely spoke of what we liked, instead concentrating on practical aspects such as size and materials—but because we had honored each other's work with our focused attention.

When I expose my young drawings in circumstances beyond my studio—however public or intimate the conditions are—I want them to go out there with courage and openness and come back to the drawing board (or iPad) with a sense of where they want to go next. As they gain confidence, whatever feedback they get will contribute to their maturity.

A
Prototype
Party

I'm not much of a hostess. I rarely have more than a few friends over at a time, let alone throw parties. But I was preparing for an upcoming exhibition, and I needed perspective. So I invited a dozen people to my studio to attend what one of my guests labeled "a focus group for art."

I was developing a multimedia exhibit with my colleague Michael Chladil, and we had been working in a vacuum. We wanted to see how people would experience and interact with the exhibit's elements in a real physical space. So, I decided to have a prototype party.

At first, I thought of this event as a crit group. But a crit is typically made up of artists who speak the same visual language. What I needed was a representation of the audience I expected at the exhibit—that is, one that was not limited to the art world.

I invited people I felt comfortable with. At this vulnerable stage of development, the last thing I needed to worry about was impressing anyone. Yes, I wanted serious feedback, but by treating this as a party (i.e., wine, snacks, and socializing), I could allow myself a more playful attitude.

The benefits of presenting our work in progress started way before the guests arrived. The question, "What should we show?" was itself daunting. First, we had to determine where we most needed feedback. Then we had to compose enough elements to be representative of the "real" exhibition.

The exhibit, titled *Overheard*, consisted of projected text and audio of cell phone conversations that would fill the gallery in varying degrees, from calmness to cacophony. For our party, we cleared the walls of my studio, and we borrowed a projector, speakers, and video monitors. As we prepared for the party showing, we uncovered new questions for the actual exhibit. Will the gallery's projectors throw a big enough image? How many conversations should we include? How much should be scripted, and how much interactive?

For our exhibition, we planned to surround visitors with a symphony of changing and overlapping sounds and images. But because we only had a subset of equipment for the party, we presented the elements sequentially. We projected, on just one wall, a series of typographic phrases with accompanying voices. Not good! Instead of being in an immersive experience, our guests essentially watched a slide show.

Early in a project, sketches and notes can be vague and hazy. They make sense to you and your colleagues, but they are indecipherable to anyone else. By attempting to translate your ideas into a tangible form for an audience, you begin to see if your intention is clear. You also become aware of meanings or connotations in the work that you had missed.

Our exhibit's content was based on overheard cell phone conversations that I had collected in Midtown Manhattan over several years. They ranged from the mundane to the dramatic, and from local accents to foreign ones. The guests at our party had strong opinions. Some wanted more entertainment, while others preferred the quotidian. Some guests wanted more diversity in the voices; others wanted longer narratives. The best part was when they interrupted the showing to tell their own stories.

The value of my friends' preferences was not in helping me to choose between drama and mundane, or diversity and storytelling. Instead, their debates made me look harder at my own assumptions and intentions. My goal was to immerse my audience in the unintentional and overlooked exposure of private conversations in public spaces. The prototype party helped to see what needed to be improved or overhauled. More importantly, it showed me where audience members were likely to complete the picture. That led me to figure out how I could support them with more interaction.

When you develop a body of artwork as an artist, you strive to achieve a balance between the early, fluid state of experimentation, and the drive toward a finished product. By exposing and articulating your ideas midway, you have time to take advantage of unexpected and fresh perspectives. If I decide to do this again, maybe I should call it a surprise party.

Curiosity
Leads

A known lefty, Leonardo da Vinci adopted "mirror writing" (right-to-left and backward) because his ideas came so rapidly that he would smudge the ink if he wrote in the normal left-to-right fashion. I learned this while viewing his *Codex on the Flight of Birds* at the Morgan Library & Museum in Manhattan.

The drawing was part of the exhibition *Leonardo da Vinci: Treasures from the Biblioteca Reale, Turin*, which also included the famous drawing *Head of a Young Woman* and the *Codex Huygens*. The show was a perfect way to see why Leonardo—whose curiosity and knowledge encompassed science, engineering, architecture, philosophy, and art—came to epitomize the Renaissance Man.

I left the Morgan uplifted. I had been feeling discouraged by our national conversation about higher education, with its emphasis on narrow learning and job-focused skills. This is the opposite of what we need to be creative thinkers and problem solvers. So, as an homage to Leonardo, I made a New Year's resolution to broaden my education and seek out widely disparate subjects, from physics to literature to history. Above all, I wanted to be guided by my curiosity instead of my résumé.

The obvious way to start was with online courses, like Khan Academy or The Great Courses. I tried both, but they languished, barely touched, on my desktop. I'm not a good online learner; I need the physicality of people and place. I looked for continuing education courses at local universities and community colleges, but again I was disappointed, because they were geared specifically toward professional development.

Then I stumbled upon Meetups.

Meetups began after 9/11 in response to the desire for community. Meetup.com is a website that facilitates ways for people worldwide who have common (and wildly diverse) interests to gather on a regular basis. Groups usually meet in public places (bars, cafés, etc.) to share activities or information about their chosen topic. Often, a Meetup announcement is a notification for an event taking place through an established club or venue, like Toastmasters (for public speaking) or the New York Society for Ethical Culture (for promoting civil society).

I dived in. My chosen subjects ranged from philosophy to astronomy, art history to drama. (I was living in New York, so there was an abundance of choices, but most cities have a lot of active and diverse groups.) I attended a philosophical discussion on privacy, a tour of the new Islamic galleries at the Metropolitan Museum of Art, and a "Behind the Scenes" workshop on the production of *King Lear*.

The New York City Public Philosophy Network (NYCPPN) believes "philosophy is most important when it helps everyday people better understand themselves and their world." The meeting was held at a bar in Midtown in the late afternoon. We began with a fifteen-minute introduction about privacy by one of the organizers; then we broke into groups. One of the participants spoke about the Panopticon, Jeremy Bentham's architectural model of the ideal prison: a design in which prisoners are never certain if they are being watched. This led to a discussion of social media, Google, the National Security Agency (NSA), and how the possibility of being watched affects one's actions. Each of us came from a different area of expertise, but with the shared curiosity of exploring privacy through the lens of philosophy.

My next Meetup event was at The Explorers Club (through the Brainiacs group) for a lecture titled "Black Holes and Gravitational

Waves." Jason Kendall, a lively speaker, helped our lay audience understand black holes, using analogies like "those socks that disappear in the dryer." He talked about Stephen Hawking's exciting discovery that his theory about black holes might be incorrect, that the holes are instead "gray," meaning that matter and energy can be temporarily held before being released back into space. In other words, those lost socks might come back. What inspired me most was that the cycle of discovery allows you to be enthusiastic about proving yourself wrong!

At the reception, while chatting with a few other guests, I asked them about the merits of a broad education in a time when it's difficult for many people to find jobs. The woman next to me said, "I work as a recruiter at an advertising agency, and to me, the most important thing is to hire people who know how to think."

This chapter favors curiosity over strictly professional development. I believe that exposure to broader knowledge will inevitably infiltrate your work. You will find the parts that are relevant and process them through your own filter. If you honor your curiosity, you will advance your career. I guarantee it.

Dear Books

My books, my books! How I've missed you!

For years, my art and design books were scattered throughout various rooms, in small bookcases, on tables, piled on the floor. Some—too many—were in storage, in cardboard boxes labeled "HEAVY."

I wanted to see them all in one place, so I finally ordered a shelving system that would cover a single large wall. My books would be available to me in one visual sweep.

When the unit was delivered and installed, I retrieved the boxes from storage. I figured it would take an afternoon, maybe two, to arrange the books on the shelves. "Not so fast!" they said to me. I had neglected them for so long, and they demanded that we get reacquainted.

Paging through one after another, I realized that their collective influence on my life comes not only from their literal contents, but also from the circumstances surrounding them. They are reminders of places, relationships, and ambitions. Where was I when I bought Matisse's *Jazz*? Who gave me *The History of Graphic Design*? How did I acquire the massive *Bauhaus*? This led to more musings: What was I doing at the time? Who were my friends, colleagues, mentors? In other words, who was I when each book came into my life?

One of my favorites is a catalogue on the work of the artist Alberto Burri. The text is in Italian, so my comprehension is fuzzy, but the memory associated with it is precise. I purchased the book during a graduate school field trip to the Fondazione Palazzo Albizzini Collezione Burri in Città di Castello. I was overwhelmed by the estate's vast spaces and evocative paintings, a feeling that has since become familiar when I encounter powerful works of art or architecture. The catalogue reminds me of this privilege—a passion that was ignited and nurtured during those years of study.

The heaviest storage box was filled with musty old typography books and actual type catalogues (remember those?) that I found during road trips to out-of-the-way bookstores. At one point, I was fixated on acquiring books by graphic designers and type designers from the early 1900s. One special find, *The Power of Print—And Men* (Mergenthaler, Linotype Company, 1936), was designed by W.A. Dwiggins; another one, *Layout in Advertising* (Harper and Brothers, 1928), was written by him. I bought these books when a designer I worked with and admired had just moved to Hingham, Massachusetts, not far from where Dwiggins had lived. I think I had intended to give him these volumes, but I never did. Now visible on my shelves, they remind me of how my colleague inspired me. I should try to find him.

My reflections made me curious about other people's experiences with their books. I started asking friends about the memories their bookshelves summoned.

A writer I've known for decades has a big house with bookcases in almost every room. Sitting in her home office, she reminisced about books that had affected her in college. She found a hardcover on a top shelf titled *Wanderer of the Wasteland*. "There was a group of cool classmates, and they were all buying and reading Zane Grey," she said. "I wanted to be like them, to emulate them, to be liked by them." I asked if she had read it. "No," she told me. "Seeing it now, I'm looking at a time in my life when I wasn't proud of myself."

Another friend showed me standouts from the shelves that she shares with her husband. At first, her selections made me laugh, because they were a litany of former boyfriends: a book on Chinese eroticism from a much older professor/lover; another by an ex-boyfriend's filmmaker brother whom my friend sought out in Paris. Then she pointed to a pair of identical books—one hardbound, one paperback: Claes Oldenburg's *Notes in Hand—Miniatures of my Notebook Pages*. "When John moved in with me," she said, "we found that we had the same book. We bonded over that, our similar taste in art." As I thumbed through the paperback, she noticed my book-envy and said, "Sorry, I can't lend one. I don't want to lose the two-ness of them."

I love seeing my books together, old sitting alongside new. Some are mangled from being carried around and dog-eared, with Post-it Notes peeking out. Others are pristine, waiting for me to get to know them. And there are the books whose meaning has changed for me, or, more surprisingly, has remained the same. When I wonder about who I was before, and who I am now, these crowded rows say, "Just look at me. I'll tell you."

Acknowledgments

My column in *Communication Arts* magazine began in 1984. Since then, I have written every year for this wonderful publication, connecting with three generations of Coynes. Their support has been present and powerful over the decades.

When I decided to collect the last thirteen years of columns into a book, I turned to Dan Tucker, founding partner of Sideshow Books. I have relied on his thoughtful guidance and expertise in making this book a tangible reality.

The sharp and insightful mind of Susan Hodara was an influence in every chapter. I am extraordinarily lucky to have her as my best friend.

Artist residencies have had a profound influence on my art making and writing—in particular, MacDowell, the American Academy in Rome, and the Women's Studio Workshop. During my stay at each, my work progressed swiftly and joyously. My students and colleagues at Harvard University, Rhode Island School of Design, and International Center of Photography provided new insights and perspectives that are now embedded in my practice.

My creative practice would not be possible without my partners in creativity—friends and colleagues from disciplines that range from writing, music, visual art, and dance, to programming and community activism, all of which merged as we erased boundaries. A lasting bond of gratitude goes to Joseph Carroll, Michael Chladil, Frank Collerius, Christine Donohue, Luba Falk Feigenberg, Allyson Greene, Jai Imbrey, Ceasar McDowell, Martha Mason, Rosanne Olson, Avani Patel, Lauren Rader, Thomas Schworer, and Tom Warren.

Nancy Weingarten, the Hodara family, and the Richmond family have been pillars of my creative work, year after year, as I wrote these chapters. Their encouragement through shared grief, growth, and happiness provided the nourishment I wanted and needed for these pages.

My brother, Bard Richmond, was, and always will be, the soul of my creative practice.

Selected Bibliography

Abramović, Marina. *The Artist Is Present*. Performance at the Museum of Modern Art, New York, March 14 to May 31, 2010.

Anelli, Marco. *Portraits in the Presence of Marina Abramović*. Bologna: Damiani, 2012.

The Artist Project. Online video series. The Metropolitan Museum of Art, New York, March 2015 to June 2016.

Baldwin, James. *Go Tell It on the Mountain*. New York: Knopf, 1953.

Brinkmann, Vinzenz, Renée Dreyfus, and Ulrike Koch-Brinkmann, eds. *Gods in Color: Polychromy in the Ancient World*. Munich: Prestel, 2017.

Burri, Alberto. *Collezione Burri*. Fondazione Palazzo Albizzini, Città di Castello, 1986.

Classen, Constance. *The Deepest Sense: A Cultural History of Touch*. Urbana: University of Illinois Press, 2012.

Cué, Elena. "Cristina Iglesias: I'm Interested in Building Places." *HuffPost*, July 7, 2017.

Doidge, Norman. *The Brain That Changes Itself: Stories of Personal Triumph from the Frontiers of Brain Science*. New York: Viking, 2007.

Drier, Thomas, and W. A. Dwiggins. *The Power of Print—and Men, 1936: Commemorating the Fifty Years of Linotype's Contribution to Printing and Publishing*. Brooklyn, NY: Mergenthaler Linotype Company, 1936.

Dwiggins, W. A. *Layout in Advertising*. New York: Harper & Brothers, 1928.

Gladstone, Brooke. "Counternarratives." Interview with John Keene. *On the Media*, WNYC, September 25, 2015.

Goldberger, Paul. *Why Architecture Matters*. New Haven: Yale University Press, 2009.

Grey, Zane. *Wanderer of the Wasteland*. New York: Harper & Brothers, 1923.

Hemingway, Ernest. *A Moveable Feast*. New York: Scribner, 1964.

Herzog, Lena. *Lost Souls*. Millbrook, New York de.MO Design Limited, 2010.

Hiss, Tony. *In Motion: The Experience of Travel*. New York: Knopf, 2010.

Kaplan, Stephen, and Rachel Kaplan. *Cognition and Environment: Functioning in an Uncertain World*. New York: Praeger, 1982.

Keene, John. *Counternarratives*. New York: New Directions, 2015.

Kendall, Jason. "Black Holes and Gravitational Waves." Lecture, The Explorers Club via Brainiacs Group, New York, October 23, 2014.

Klee, Paul. *Pedagogical Sketchbook*. New York: Praeger, 1953.

Koch, Kenneth. "One Train May Hide Another." In *One Train: Poems by Kenneth Koch*, 3–4. New York: Knopf, 1994.

Lahiri, Jhumpa. "Teach Yourself Italian." *The New Yorker*, December 7, 2015.

Leonardo, da Vinci. *Codex on the Flight of Birds*. n.p., 1505 to 1506

Maclear, Christy, and Dorothy Dunn. *The Glass House*. New York: Assouline; National Trust for Historic Preservation, 2008.

Matisse, Henri. *Jazz*. George Braziller, 1992.

Meggs, Philip B. *A History of Graphic Design*. New York: Wiley, 1998.

Messner, Ann. *The Free Library and Other Histories*. Self-published exhibition catalog, 2018.

Oldenburg, Claes. *Notes in Hand—Miniatures of My Notebook Pages*. New York: E.P. Dutton and Company, 1971.

Oliver, Mary. "Wild Geese." In *Dream Work*, 14–15. Boston: Atlantic Monthly Press, 1986.

Ono, Yoko. *Cut Piece*. Film, Carnegie Recital Hall, 1965. Essay in *Bungei Shunjū*, 1974.

Proust, Marcel. *Remembrance of Things Past*. Vol. I. *Swann's Way & Within a Budding Grove*. Translated by C. K. Scott Moncrieff. New York: Random House, 1934.

Prose, Francine. *Reading Like a Writer: A Guide for People Who Love Books and for Those Who Want to Write Them*. New York: HarperCollins, 2006.

Sacks, Oliver. *The Mind's Eye*. New York: Knopf, 2010.

Seinfeld, Jerry. "Interview: How to Write a Joke." *The New York Times*, December 20, 2012.

Simon, Peter Angelo. *Muhammad Ali: Fighter's Heaven 1974*. London: Reel Art Press, 2016.

Sontag, Susan. *On Photography*. New York: Farrar, Straus and Giroux, 1977.

Talbot, Margaret. "The Myth of Whiteness in Classical Sculpture." *The New Yorker*, October 29, 2018.

Tharp, Twyla. *The Creative Habit: Learn It and Use It for Life*. New York: Simon & Schuster, 2003.

Turkle, Sherry. *Alone Together: Why We Expect More from Technology and Less from Each Other*. New York: Basic Books, 2011.

Twombly, Robert, ed *Frederick Law Olmsted: Essential Texts*. New York: W. W. Norton & Company, 2010.

West, Thomas G. *In the Mind's Eye: Visual Thinkers, Gifted People With Dyslexia and Other Learning Difficulties, Computer Images and the Ironies of Creativity*. Amherst, NY: Prometheus Books, 1997.

Wingler, Hans M. *Bauhaus: Weimar, Dessau, Berlin, Chicago*. Cambridge, MA: MIT Press, 1969.

Woolf, Virginia. *Mrs. Dalloway*. London: Hogarth Press, 1925.

Yoko Ono: One Woman Show, 1960–1971. New York: Museum of Modern Art, New York, May 17 to September 7, 2015.

Index